W9-BWF-182

Teaching & Joy

Edited by
Robert Sornson
and
James Scott

ASCD

Association for Supervision and Curriculum Development
Alexandria, Virginia

Association for Supervision and Curriculum Development • 1250 N. Pitt Street • Alexandria, Virginia 22314-1453, USA • Telephone: 1-800-933-2723 or 703-549-9110; Fax: 703-299-8631

Gene R. Carter, *Executive Director*

Michelle Terry, *Assistant Executive Director, Program Development*

Ronald S. Brandt, *Assistant Executive Director*

Nancy Modrak, *Director, Publishing*

Julie Houtz, *Managing Editor of Books*

Margaret A. Oosterman, *Associate Editor*

NiKette Banks, *Project Assistant*

Gary Bloom, *Director, Design, Editorial, and Production Services*

Karen Monaco, *Senior Designer*

Tracey A. Smith, *Production Coordinator*

Dina Murray, *Production Assistant*

Valerie Sprague, *Desktop Publisher*

Printed in the United States of America.   ASCD Stock No. 196076

ASCD member price: $13.95; nonmember price: $16.95   s4/97

Library of Congress Cataloging-in-Publication Data
    Teaching and joy / edited by Robert Sornson and James Scott.
        p. cm.
        Contents: Richard / Harlan Rimmerman — The first 30 years are the hardest : notes from the yellow brick road / Mimi Brodsky Chenfeld — Driving Master Brian / David Weikart — Teaching and flower power / Ron Wallen — More alike than different / Nora Martin — Memories of elementary laughter / Steve Wilson — Miss Daisy / Donald Davis — How to give your kids an unfair advantage / Jim Fay — Reflections of joy / Virginia McClary Delatte — Magic / Carolyn Mamchur — Increase your laugh life! / Sheila Feigelson — Learning that came alive on Heartbreak Hill / Judy-Arin Krupp — Child's play : making molehills out of mountains / Allen Klein — The birthday card / Caryn Edwards — Find your joy by following your heart / Deborah Rozman — Joy in valuing / Sidney Simon — Downhill skiing / Robert Sornson — Meet my first mentor / Lois Wolfe-Morgan — Impact / Guy Vander Jagt — Ignite the joy within! / Valla Dana Fotiades — Journey of trust and joy / Mary Gayle Floden — Discovering purpose / Rick Scott — An interview with Bernie Siegel, M.D. / Robert Sornson — The heart radiates / Shinichi Suzuki — Forty-nine years later / Al Fialka.
        ISBN 0-87120-271-9 (pbk.)
        1. Teachers—United States.   2. Teaching—United States.
    I. Sornson, Robert.   II. Scott, James, 1948–
    LB1775.2.T477   1997
    371.102—DC21
                               97-4642
                               CIP

01   00   99   98   97   5   4   3   2   1

"TEACHING AND JOY"

If not for you,

bring joy into the lives of your teachers.

If not for you,

bring joy into the lives of your students and their families.

If not for you,

bring joy into the lives of your peers.

Better yet,

bring joy into your own life.

—ANONYMOUS

Teaching and Joy

Introduction

We hope you receive this book as a blessing. May your schools, classrooms, and homes be filled with joy. Real joy. The kind you experience when spending time with others who share your sense of purpose and common commitment to the love and growth of children.

Throughout our land, homes and schools are filled with a tangible joy. You can see it, feel it, and hear it when you walk into a great school or a loving home. Not the momentary joy of amusement, but the life-sustaining, heartfelt joy of those who feel privileged to contribute to the development of youngsters.

Have you ever seen a master craftsperson at work? They move easily and deliberately, and cannot be flustered or hurried. Master teachers are the same, heart and brain working in sync, centered by their clear purpose. They share the same joy as their students when absorbed in meaningful learning, feeling its inherent quality and value.

To those who advocate school improvement and reform, as we do, please consider two things. Schools are working harder and accomplishing more than ever. And, all school improvement initiatives might well be examined from the perspective of whether they will add to, or detract from, joyous teaching and learning experiences in the classroom.

Whether whole language or TQM, integrated thematic instruction or vision training, educational initiatives should enhance the quality of joy in our schools. We must advocate for improvements and initiatives that consider the importance of maintaining a spirit of joy within the teachers, students, and parents.

We hope the stories, articles, and vignettes in *Teaching and Joy* will reinforce the perspective that great learning and great teaching can occur only in an atmosphere of love, clear purpose, and commitment. To us, that describes an atmosphere of joy. Our authors remind us to value and protect the joy in our hearts and homes and schools. If this book helps recapture your own joyous

sense of teaching or learning, then we have truly accomplished our objective. May you look upon all of life's teaching and learning experiences through eyes of joy.

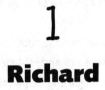

Richard

BY HARLAN RIMMERMAN

The start of my third year teaching 5th grade at Mt. View School was one that would change my life. Richard was assigned to my class. He was smaller in stature than most of the other boys, but a real fighter—he would back down from no one. Because Richard was often bored from being unable to do his assignment, he was also adept at getting into trouble. Classified as a nonreader, he had become one of those students passed on year to year because teachers did not want him in their classes.

Richard and I had a rough start. We both battled to see who would control the class, and I barely won. Yet, when two people battle, respect and a wary friendship may develop between them, as it did between Richard and me. Over time, I learned that he was from a single-parent home. Dad had left years ago, and Mom and little brother lived at home with Mom's new boyfriend. Fortunately for Richard, the boyfriend took a liking to both boys and treated them quite well.

Richard missed very little school, was usually neat and clean, but struggled academically. He would try hard and then become so frustrated that I would see tears well up in his eyes. Richard was a fighter—he wouldn't quit. But the previous years of being told he was a troublemaker and not very smart had taken their toll.

One Monday morning, Richard came running into the classroom full of excitement. "Mr. Rim," he shouted, "we went to the wrestling matches Saturday night and I got this magazine that my 'dad' bought me. It's got a lot of neat stories in it."

At first, I just stood there, talking to Richard about his weekend. Then I was struck by the thunderbolt of recollection—Richard saying, "it has a lot of neat stories in it."

"Richard," I replied in a daze, "tell me about some of these stories." Richard opened the magazine to the first story and told me about the "big match" and what had happened. I took the magazine, flipped through several more pages, and asked about the story located near the middle of the magazine. Again, he gave me a beautiful, detailed report. I knew he must have read the stories to be able to tell me about them in depth. I looked at Richard and realized at the same moment he did that he was a reader. Richard knew from the smile on my face how I felt, and when I saw that beautiful smile come to his face, I knew he would never be the same.

Richard did indeed become a reader. Not from anything I did, but solely by accident, a fate of good luck. He had found for himself what we call intrinsic motivation. I was just lucky enough to be there at the right time to help him realize what had happened—that inside his brain, programmed to think it wasn't worth anything, the circuits had come together to make a megaconnection letting Richard know he could be successful in school and in life. As the year went on, my expectations for Richard kept increasing, and at the same time, Richard met new and more wonderful successes. He was one of my favorites and now, even 10 years later, I often think of him when I see another child struggling.

I lost track of Richard when I moved out of town, but I stopped worrying about him because I knew on that one beautiful day at Mt. View School, when he brought me the magazine, that Richard was going to be all right.

Richard

Harlan Rimmerman is the Assistant Superintendent for the Ft. Leavenworth, Kansas, School District. He is also the facilitator of the ASCD Cooperative Learning Network. Rimmerman has been a classroom teacher at both the elementary and secondary levels, a building principal, and a central office administrator. He is also a national trainer in the areas of cooperative learning and accelerated learning.

Rimmerman's professional training was from the University of Nebraska and the University of Kansas. His philosophy of education is that "bottom-line, decisions should be made based upon what is best for kids."

Teaching—beyond all things—requires a commitment to basic ideas, an attitude of learning, and a focus on what works with children. Never give up on a child. Within each child lives a prodigy. Mimi Chenfeld reminds us of some important rules about teaching and joy.

2

The First 30 Years Are the Hardest: Notes from the Yellow Brick Road

BY MIMI BRODSKY CHENFELD

I visited with Sister Miriam at an education conference. We are old conference friends. She is probably one of the last nuns in America to wear her old habit. And, she never dropped her other old habits, such as lovingness, caring, playfulness, sharing.

I whispered, "Sister Miriam, this is my 30th year of teaching!"

She returned the confidence, "This is my 60th! The first 30 years are the hardest!" (I planted a tree for her in Israel in honor of her 60th year of teaching.)

Source: From *Young Children* (March 1987). Copyright © 1987 by the National Association for the Education of Young Children. Reprinted by permission of the publisher.

A child asked, "How long have you been a teacher?"

"30 years."

"Well," the child concluded, "you must know how to do it by heart."

**These are notes from the heart as we journey along the Yellow
Brick Road in search of Oz, Kansas, The Wizard, Courage, Brains,
Heart. In search of . . .**

I met a teacher I hadn't seen for many years. He asked if I was still teaching.
"Of course," I answered.

His eyes showed surprise.

"I'm going to keep trying until I get it right!"

**These are notes from the journey as we bump along, losing and
finding our way, stopping at scenic routes, detouring at danger spots,
speeding along on cruise control, plunging into the traffic snarls.
Notes from the heart . . . Notes from the start . . .**

I started teaching second graders on a stage in the gym of a shabby, over-
crowded school in upstate New York in 1956. We had a teacher shortage in
America then. We had few materials. No high-interest, low-vocabulary, shiny
books. No colorful filmstrips, overhead projectors, opaques, video libraries, or
Apple™ computers.

Just apples, the kids, and us.

Since that time, I've worked with toddlers to senior citizens, from Head
Start to Upward Bound, from gifted and talented to learning disabled, from
overachievers to underachievers, from ghettos to suburbs, from New York to
Hawaii. The things I believed then, I believe now—only stronger. Now my beliefs are as solid as the House Made Out of Bricks (Yellow Brick Road? House
Made Out of Bricks? Oh well, these are just *notes*.) They started out flimsy, easy
to blow over, almost as fragile as the House Made Out of Straw. But time and
children helped me to turn the straw into bricks. No wolf or wind can blow this

5

house over. I believe in loving children, in loving *people*. I believe in caring, playfulness, sharing, courage. . .

All of my T-shirts are reading materials. Some of the messages printed on my shirts read:

> "I am still learning." (Michelangelo's motto)
> "Teaching is one of the few professions that permits love."
> (Roethke)
> "The lesson that is not enjoyed is not learned." (Talmud)

I was driving to an AEYC conference in Canfield, Ohio. The directions Muriel sent me were excellent, clear as calligraphy. I followed them to the letter. I got lost. Totally, dismally lost. I asked and followed, understood and misunderstood. I ended up in a phone booth outside of a restaurant and called Muriel.

"This is where I am. I don't know where it is. Come and meet me!"

Muriel was astonished. "You're only a mile away. But, it's impossible for you to be at *that* restaurant if you followed my directions!"

We in education know the impossible is our everyday agenda.

There are many ways to reach our destinations. Sometimes, the way prescribed is *not* the way that succeeds. We have our educational goals, our directives, our curriculum guidelines. Often, we are given preset ways to accomplish those goals. Sometimes those ways don't work. We mustn't think there is only *one* approach. But if goals, approaches, and curriculum grow out of children's ages, stages, interests, and feelings, they are more *likely* to work. Even so, we mustn't think there *is* only one approach.

A Native American saying goes something like this: "Let all the paths recognize each other."

Recently, I worked with children in a city school under their Artists-in-the-Schools program. I walked into one of the rooms while the children were at recess. This gave me a few minutes to explore before they came back. The walls of this room were papered with *rules*: If You Do This, THAT Will Happen to You; If You Dare to Do this Twice, THESE Things Will Be Your Punishment, and so on.

Each item was very, very specific—Sit in *this* position, line up in *that* location. The rules covered every waking moment, every behavior possibility. I expected the world's most obedient, cooperative, courteous students. Instead, I was almost trampled by rude, rough, mean-spirited children running, fighting, and shouting into the room.

This group of students was one of the most difficult I have worked with. I was dismayed by their behavior.

After our session, I had a chance to spend a few minutes with their teacher, who frustratedly told me, "these are the toughest students I have taught in 10 years of teaching."

I looked at her room of ignored rules and collective rudeness and responded honestly, from the gut.

"If something isn't working, don't keep doing it."

We talked for a while. I shared my feelings. "These rules aren't working with *these* kids. Every class is a special mix of specific individuals. Every year is a new year. Maybe nothing you have ever studied or learned will work with this particular group of children. You'll have to try everything—known and unknown—old and new, borrowed and blue, to find ways to reach them. What do they care about? What do they respond to? What touches them? What are their interests? When are they most responsive? What's on their magic vocabulary list? Who are their heroes?"

As I left, a child slipped me a note. It read: "Please don't leave us."

There are no unreachable children. Only those who are, as yet, unreached.

I still believe as I always believed—there are no unreachable children. Only those who are, as yet, unreached. That is a leap of faith. As we believe, so we teach. In my House of Bricks a tapestry hangs. Sewn on the fabric is the Edwin Markham poem:

> He drew a circle that shut me out
> Heretic, rebel, a thing to flout.
> But *love* and I had the wit to win
> We drew a circle that took him in.

I think that poem is the core of what education is all about. The great teachers I know are circle drawers. They never accept being left out nor agree to leave a child out. They continuously make larger and larger circles to take in an alienated child, to turn a child from OFF to ON, to help a child who knows only failure taste success, to change the history of a child with a broken self-image. Never give up on a child. On children. Sometimes, you may be the *only* person who hasn't given up, even with a very young child! Sometimes you are the only person making that leap of faith, the only person believing in that child.

I have lived through 30 years of acronyms: EMR, G&T, USSR, LD, VC. I am one of those primitive people who thought VC was a new program designed to help us understand the Viet Cong. Did I guess it meant *Values Clarification*? You mean we only began clarifying values when we adopted the letters for a new acronym? I thought we *always* clarified values from the twitch of the lips to the boost of an eyebrow; from the smirk on our face to the ice in our eyes; from saying nothing to saying everything, we clarify values. We always have.

The message on a poster read: "The Best Way To Send an Idea Is To Wrap It Up In a Person." The best way to clarify values is to live those values every day, to demonstrate those values in everything we do. And *I* value loving, caring, playfulness, sharing, courage. . . .

Stop on the scenic route and spend time with teachers like Ronni who teaches special education. She's a shouter, a screamer, a laugher, a hugger, a

lover, a friend, a taskmaster. No doubts about where she stands on the major issues of the day. She votes LIFE all the way!

She tells kids who have had numerous experiences with failures, "You are
not going to fail in my class. Even if you try, I won't let you! Do you hear me? I
won't permit it! You are going to succeed (or else)." She cajoles, threatens, rewards, jokes, tickles, celebrates. Her kids succeed.

All education should be *special.*

Another idea written on the walls of my House Made Out of Bricks is the
Yiddish proverb, "All of my children are prodigies." That's under VC. Or is it TLC?

If you believe it and live it every day, you'll find that it's true. I have never
had a child who did not demonstrate originality, creativity, imagination, surpris-
ing talents. The children are all there waiting for you to believe in them, to expect the *best* from them. In this high-tech, high-anxiety, computer-crazed,
supercharged decade, they need you to hallow them more than ever. Through it
all, do you have the courage?

I did a workshop with education majors who were student-teaching. They
were sharing projects. One team reported on an outstanding zoo project that
took weeks of writing, reading, researching, math, art, and science—all the curriculum strands interwoven (as all good education weaves). One of the sub-
topics was a listing of endangered species that the 8-year-old children had
researched. The university student-teachers read off the list. I felt my hand
raise and heard myself say, "There's one endangered species you forgot—*the
spirits of children."*

I'm worried about our children. In our pressure-cooker system, many of
them are learning earlier than ever to be failures, to lose faith in themselves, to
feel inhibited, squelched, defeated, discouraged, closed off, anxious, apathetic.

Frayda and Miriam, dance teachers in an Artists-in-the-Schools program,
shared music and dance with children in a school for physically challenged students. In keeping with mainstreaming, a class of "normal" children came to the
program with their teacher, who turned out to be a very uptight, stern, joyless

person. Miriam and Frayda drummed, chanted, talked, and sang. They invited the children to join them. From all corners of the gym, kids in wheelchairs, on crutches, in braces, limped, rolled, hobbled, and crawled eagerly to participate. Only the "normal" children, frozen in their seats by their teacher's strict stare, never moved. *Which children were handicapped?*

The director of a preschool and her staff took a day off to visit another program in the city. They observed young children learning in silence with minimal interaction, passive lessons, formal instruction, and ditto sheets galore. When the children went to the restroom, they walked in single file with their hands on top of their heads. Talking wasn't allowed.

That night, my friend watched a program on TV about Prisoners of War. She gasped as she watched the men walk single file, hands on top of their heads. Talking wasn't allowed.

In the 1990s, we still have classrooms of harsh silence, of fear.

The spirits of our children are an endangered species.

I want to launch a nationwide anti-smug campaign. I am meeting more and more children who already know everything!

"We already studied colors!" "We had the human body in second grade!"

"We did nutrition last year!" (I told them about the scientist Dr. McClintock who has been studying kernels of corn on the cob for 60 years and she hasn't finished corn yet.)

I asked a group of kids if they had been following Halley's comet. They answered, "We finished the Solar System." I'm worried about the shrinking of minds, the closing of doors and windows, the shriveling of curiosity and wonder.

As I believe, so I teach. Educators and parents, join the anti-smug campaign! Down with convergent thinking, closed absolute right-and-wrong answers! Up with divergent thinking, open-ended exploring, brainstorming, wonder-full discussions and questions!

Let's preserve the minds and spirits of our students and ourselves as fiercely as we fight to preserve endangered species like baby seals and whales.

My notes read: *"Trust your instincts."*

"The greatest technique in the universe is the technique in the human heart." (Margolit Ovid)

I visited Brenda's class of young authors. Her kids were in a group hug, Brenda in the middle. She beamed as she announced, "Mimi, these are the most talented, creative, delightful writers. Every one of them is imaginative and original. Now, Charles sometimes has to have his work translated from the original. . ."

Charles grinned and showed me one of his original papers. Totally indecipherable. Any but a life-affirming, loving teacher would have tossed it into the nearest wastepaper basket with a barrage of scolding gunfire. But Brenda found a "technique" to help him succeed and improve without ever losing faith in himself. He proudly shared his second rewritten paper—clearer, neater. At the bottom of the page, he signed, "Translated from the original by Charles."

Dawn is another teacher who has a love affair with her students. They come from the inner city, from single-parent homes, from English as a second language. Her children come to school when they're sick. They don't want to miss a minute. In some classes, children come to school well and *get* sick.

One of Dawn's students asked her, "Do you know what my four favorite things in the world are?"

Dawn couldn't guess.

"Number one is school. Number two is school. Number three is school. Number four is school."

Mary Sue, a movement educator, visited a class for a day. Later, she received a letter from one of the children.

"Thank you for coming today. You made me happy for the rest of my life."

Teaching & Joy

I n my House Made Out of Bricks, in my journey on the Yellow Brick Road, I've come more and more to the conclusion that there are only two choices in education. Life and Death! If you are undecided, indifferent, neutral, apathetic, you are on the side of Death. Death of ideas, of excitement, of discovery. Death of the spirit.

If you are on the side of Life, you can't go wrong. Oh, you can make mistakes, lose your way, misunderstand your goals, misinterpret directions, but you can't go wrong with children who know you love them and are committed to their welfare, to their minds, to their healthy growth. Dedicated to the sacredness of your precious time together.

Rhoda took her preschoolers for a field trip and got lost. They wandered around for a while looking for the right place. Rhoda was flustered, embarrassed. When they finally found their destination, 4-year-old Peter beamed his shining smile up at her and burst, "We're very proud of you."

T here are more notes than space. There are more notes than time to write them all. There are so many life-filled teachers, principals, parents, childcare workers, children on the journey, walking with us, lighting our way, enriching the trip. I could fill a book with their names alone.

I am lucky to know them and feel their warmth. In our field, sometimes our light and warmth get buried beneath a barrage of instructional strategies, methods, and materials. Sister Miriam, I'm at the 30-year mark. I see you ahead, rainbow bright and glistening. As early childhood educators—*as human beings*— we are all on the Yellow Brick Road seeking Courage, Brains, and Heart. Like Dorothy, Tin Man, Scarecrow, and Lion, we already have these gifts, but we don't always know it. We forget a lot. In spite of pressures to the contrary, we need to dig out our courage to teach in ways that are loyal to the spirits of young children.

I agree with the Tin Man who said, "Brains are not the best thing in the world. Once I had brains and a heart also; having tried them both, I would much rather have a heart."

These are notes from the heart.

Mimi Brodsky Chenfeld of Columbus, Ohio, is a teacher, writer, and national consultant. She is the author of Teaching Language Arts Creatively *(2nd ed.) and* Creative Experiences for Young Children *(both published by Harcourt Brace Jovanovich).* The National Association for the Education of Young Children (NAEYC) *published a collection of her essays,* Teaching in the Key of Life.

She possesses that wonderful gift shared by every great teacher—joy—in her life, her beliefs, and her work. That joy pulsates through her writing as it must pulsate through her classroom. A 3rd grader wrote to her: "Mimi, you're the queen of fun."

For the last 25 years, Dave Weikart has had a significant influence on the education of young children. Quiet rides in the morning with his young grandson remind him of some of the most important lessons he's learned about great teaching and learning.

3

Driving Master Brian

BY DAVID WEIKART

Each morning around 7:45, I drive to my daughter's house to gather my grandson, Brian, for our trip to the High/Scope demonstration preschool. If you have not spent a daily, 45-minute drive with a 3-year-old and been a grandfather at the same time, you don't know the pleasure. There are so many things to discuss: "I went with my dad to Big Wheel, and we got some new baskets for my room"; to observe: "Hey, Pa, the horses are still out in the yard in the cold. See the steam"; and to wonder about, which is the topic I want to share with you.

About 10 minutes into the ride, we pass a rather small microwave tower, with only two dishes and a single blinking light on top of its 100-foot height. For the first several months of fall, Brian didn't notice it, although the tower is

fairly close to the road. But one morning, he fairly jumped with joy as the drive started. He and his mom had seen "flying pancakes" the day before on their ride home, and he wanted to show me. Brian was very excited about his new discovery and couldn't wait for me to see—pancakes, lights, and all.

As we drew near the tower, the red light at the top was blinking steadily, and I "wondered" why the light was on. Brian immediately told me, because "it's a little bit sprinklin'," which it was. Over the next several weeks, the light was on because it was "a little bit winter," or because "there is snow on the ground," or occasionally "because it is a little bit dark."

This event became the high point of the trip, when we would "wonder" and verify whether the light would be on or off. On bright sunny mornings, Brian would confidently predict that the light would be on because of some generally true condition, such as winter. On dark mornings, Brian would predict the light would be on because of the dark. But holding degrees of "lightness" in his mind was not yet possible.

Then, one morning in mid-January, Brian announced that the light was off because it was "too light." After a pause, he added that it was "still a little bit winter." By February, he had sorted it out and predicted accurately on the basis of the degree of light or dark.

Aside from the fun and suspense this small mystery provided Brian each day, a larger educational purpose was served. Brian entertained a problem each day, predicted an outcome, held it in mind, and verified his position based on his direct observation. Being right or wrong never entered the picture as a function of adult input; describing the solution was always Brian's prerogative. Using various explanations based on what else he was observing allowed him to gradually create the "degree of lightness" as an explanation. Early on, Brian understood that something happened because something caused it to happen. But aside from that logical framework, he felt free to invent whatever seemed appropriate at the time. Telling Brian the rule and then drilling him each day would have been easy. But then I would have missed that excited, wondrous cry of, "Pa, it's on!" as we came around the bend.

Teaching & Joy

Who really cares whether or not Brian knows the rules of when microwave tower lights are on? The real function of this interaction is to create and support a process essential to the success of any child in becoming an independent thinker. Further, Brian learned that adults he values also "wonder" about things. The right and wrong here was always tied to his own prediction, not to remembering some rule and then waiting for the adult to verify the application.

A second odd thing has been unfolding in our daily drives. Between the towns of Clinton and Saline is a traditional Michigan farmhouse, with a busy highway separating the farm barns from the residence. On a slope near the barns are five or six light-colored boulders large enough to be—well—pigs.

"Hey, Brian, look at all those pigs!" I remark. "That big one has its snout way deep in the ground!"

Brian looks at the stones, frowns, looks again, and says, "Pa, those are not pigs. They're stones. The pigs are in the barn."

Several weeks go by, with the "stones-that-are-pigs" discussion coming up frequently. I must be careful not to let my joke become a problem to this literal 3-year-old. But about the same time the microwave tower mystery gets resolved, Brian announces as we pass one day, "Hey, Pa. They're your pigs. Mine are in the barn because it's cold." As I glance at him, he is looking directly at me with a huge "gotcha" smile on his face.

At Brian's age, things can be funny, but jokes are hard to accept and harder yet to return. Things must be clearly understood before they can be joked about. With the light on the microwave tower, Brian was wrestling with a concrete experience to reach a working hypothesis. With the stone pigs, the reverse was presented, denying what he sees. He solved it by giving ownership over to me and by beginning to see the humor.

In our classrooms at High/Scope, adults are trained to ask questions. As with the microwave tower light, our questions can be problem setting, with the verification left to the child. With the pigs, the issue is to reverse roles of the grandpa, who knows nothing about pigs, with the child, who can clearly verify the error. Through both of these examples, the issue sets the stage for the child to think independently. The answers are irrelevant—the process is of primary

importance. Because parents and grandparents have more individual time with children, they are important allies in helping children become independent learners.

Some days I find it tough to drive Master Brian to school. Turning on the radio, passing time without comment, and thinking my own thoughts instead of being concerned with the needs of a 3-year-old would be easier. How easy to be directive, to control, and to explain. But the rewards of role-playing (our little brown pickup "talks" to each passing school bus, which returns the compliment); singing ("Little Red Caboose" and "She'll be Coming Round the Mountain" are the current favorites); observing animal life (the four Clydesdale horses and the three muskrat houses in the farm pond); and hearing about the involved conversations concerning family, friends, and school happenings more than compensate for the effort. And while indirectly "teaching" my small grandson, I joyously stumble into relearning many of life's mysteries.

David Weikart is President of High/Scope Educational Research Foundation in Ypsilanti, Michigan, a nonprofit research, development, and training organization. His responsibilities include serving as Director of the High/Scope Perry Preschool Project. Started in 1962, the project studies long-term results of high-quality early childhood education on the growth and development of young children through adulthood. Weikart is also coordinator of the International Association for the Evaluations of Educational Achievement (IEA) Preprimary Study. This 15-nation study looks at 4-year-olds in and out of home care, and the relationship of their experiences to achievement in formal schooling.

Weikart was a member of the National Commission on Children, established by the president and Congress. He has lectured at international meetings in Europe and Asia.

A graduate of Oberlin College and the University of Michigan, Weikart has written numerous books and articles on such topics as early childhood education, special education, and curriculum development.

Are you fascinated by the people in your life? To be fascinated is a decision you make, which determines how you look at life and how you enjoy your work.

4

Teaching and Flower Power

BY RON WALLEN

Please, I urge you to read the following list carefully. Here are some of the best teachers on earth:

Miss Mary Graves (without doubt, the greatest school administrator who ever lived), The Honorable Ronald Belt, and Mr. Willard Wallen, all of Macon, Missouri; Ms. Marjorie Wilkerson-Foreman, of Novelty, Missouri; Mr. Walt Webber, of Columbia, Missouri; Mrs. Deloma Thompson, of Kirsville, Missouri; The Rev. Clyde Miller, Miss Helen Naughton, and Mrs. Bernice Maitland, all of La Plata, Missouri; Mr. Tom Hill, of Lake St. Louis, Missouri; Dr. John B. Alexander and Dr. Fred Helsabeck, both of Canton, Missouri; Dr. Lorenzo Green, of Jefferson City, Missouri; Dr. Bruce M. Metzger, Dr. Hugh T. Kerr, Dr. Diogenes Allen, Dr. Walter Kaufmann, and Ms. Lisa Zobian, all of Princeton, New Jersey; Dr. Louise Courtois and Dr. Bryant M. Kirkland, both of New York City;

Dr. Norman Pittenger, of Cambridge, England; and Dr. Harold Oliver, of Boston, Massachusetts.

This list covers only the first twenty-some years of my life. Five on the list have died, and I am uncertain where four of the other seventeen are. I am certain, however, of one thing: These 22 people are present in every part of my life, every day. They continue to teach me and inform my most significant decisions as I draw on their respect for learning and, more important, their respect for learners. Most of the 22 may be classified as professional educators, but not all. There is a minister, a real estate executive, a judge, a grandfather, and someone who cared when no one else seemed to.

As odd as it sounds coming from someone who has spent as much time as I have in formal educational settings, learning is hard for me. I have to work very hard to learn and synthesize new material, and I get unbelievably bored in the process. Yet, I love to learn and always have. These teachers are the reason why. From the time I entered 1st grade, all the way through postdoctoral work, these teachers on my list refused to let me get left behind because I did not at first understand, could not see, or was simply slow (or "lazy"). In those instances when I was way out in front, they moved ahead to challenge me.

These 22 teachers had one wonderful thing in common: Each understood that people are like flowers—they may come in bunches, but they are beautiful one at a time. Put differently, these teachers recognized that people may appear in groups, but they disappear one lost individual at a time. Each of these teachers had the wisdom to realize that very few people do anything according to someone else's schedule. The teacher can make the rules for the race, but the student must set the pace. Teaching is about reaching; the material is immaterial unless it materializes in the mind of each individual student. The output of the teacher is measured solely by the outcome in the student.

When the going gets tough, all it takes to succeed is one person to understand your unique way of learning and your individual interests and strengths, and to help you believe in your own capabilities, which is what these extraordinary teachers did for me. Respect for the individual learner took precedence over "the class," "the lesson," "the assignment," "the test," even "the law" and administrative policy. What mattered most to these teaching masters was that I heard, not that they were speaking. The result of this kind of teacher-respect was that I received powerful and much-needed boosts to my self-worth.

Self-Esteem and Joy

Positive self-worth comes from two things; both are the natural outgrowth of the influence of great teachers: being respected as an individual by someone in a power position, and discovering one's own power through personal accomplishment and discipline. When one's teachers are wise and talented enough to see that both these things occur, instead of education being a drudgery or necessary evil imposed on the learner by outside forces, it becomes an inner experience of sheer joy. I learned to love learning and to love myself learning. Happiness is an empowered teacher.

These teachers taught me that education, at its best, places the needs and progress of the individual student ahead of preconceived programs or standardized evaluations. Anything less—in the name of policy, lesson plans, rules, a parent's desire to create a superachiever, fear that natural exuberance will lead to uncontrollable behavior, frustration that the subject matter will not get covered properly, even concern for teamwork or commitment to "community action"—is worse than poor teaching methods; it is inhuman. The only reason to teach anybody anything is to increase that learner's potential, enjoyment, and respect for being uniquely human. We are not vegetables, we are not beasts of the field, and we are not computers. We are human beings. Yes, we have a serious responsibility for how we treat plants, animals, and our entire ecosystem. And we have a responsibility for how we live together on this planet. But our first concern had better be how respectfully we interact with and educate one another, one single human being at a time.

Each person is an original, a biological work of art. Historically, every attempt to place the so-called welfare of the group above respect for the individual has resulted in pain for most people, as well as ultimate cultural and economic decline for the society in general. Individuals must be treated with supreme respect, or else any talk of the importance of the "group" or the "whole" is a lie. Respect is the watchword; joy for learning is the result.

Joy in learning results when the learner is respected. Respect for the learner is present only when we demonstrate empathy for each individual's unique strengths, weaknesses, problems, and progress. Without enthusiasm and respect for the individual, a teacher is simply not teaching. Why? Because teaching is one human being influencing the mind and emotions of another human being. That interaction can only happen when the unique humanity of each student is paramount to the teacher.

Let's Get Real

The challenge to any teacher, however, comes when confronted with real-life students and their behaviors in situations where needs and numbers swell to overflowing. Even the best teacher (e.g., professional classroom educator, activities director at a retirement community, physician with her patients, army general with his troops, coach with her team, trainer with corporate managers, father teaching daughter to bake cookies or mother demonstrating what calmness looks like to her 2-year-old son) has times when patience strains, enthusiasm ebbs, and creative juices run sour.

Those of us who teach need to consciously nourish our own joy and energy for what we do. Our commitments to those we teach are too important to leave this nourishment to chance. We must proactively guard against letting the job, the grind of daily schedules, or the apathy and negativity of certain people we cannot avoid diminish our zest for teaching and our enthusiasm for the individuals we teach.

The big question, of course, is, How do you do that? How do you keep yourself sharp, keenly interested in the material, inspired by the challenge of teaching, and intrigued by the uniqueness of each student? How do you make sure that, as the horticulturist might say, you never go to seed? How do you kindle and rekindle the joy of teaching? In other words, how do you keep the bloom on your passion for life and work? There are many answers to those questions.

None, however, make the point better than the metaphor of the flower. To me, flowers are much like people.

I love flowers. I like to plant flowers, watch them grow, take care of them, feed them, and wonder which ones will be back again next year. I enjoy wild flowers, tame flowers, house flowers, and flowers in the meadow. I particularly applaud a rugged weed with a colorful face and a creative corolla, trying to move up in the world by passing itself off as a flowering lovely. More often than not, the weed can pull it off, provided it catches the eye of a child and eludes the judgment of an expert. I should mention also that I don't like flower shows very much. I think flowers take themselves too seriously at flower shows. But, like people who take themselves too seriously, such flowers are still fun to look at, and they do add to the interesting diversity of life.

Flower Power

Flowers are wonderful. Flowers have power. They have the power to teach. Flowers show and tell us what it takes to make our short season on this earth a thing of beauty. The lessons are legion; the ones I have chosen for you here are tailor-made to remind you that it is natural to give the world your best, and to enjoy yourself in the process:

• **Succeed as a seed.** A seed is created for one single purpose: to grow. So are you. Unless you continue adding to your own life, you cannot keep adding to the lives of the people around you. This effort requires nourishment. I am amazed by how many people pay lip service to personal growth and yet are basically the same today, especially attitudinally, as they were 10 years ago. They haven't continued to nourish themselves with new ideas; challenged themselves by seriously questioning old ways of doing things; and creatively brought together people, information, and programs heretofore unrelated. Further, the only way you as a teacher may expect someone else to grow is if you are willing to lead the way. Productivity expert and author of *Quality Without Tears*, Philip Crosby once said, "What should be obvious from the outset is that people perform to the standards of their leaders." Make no mistake about it, as a

teacher you are a leader. The only way your admonition to others to "keep studying, keep growing" will have any moral authority is if they see that you are doing the same yourself. The healthiest people in the world are those who can still get excited about what they have yet to learn, see, and do. The most successful people are those who know that the human mind is a seed that, once germinated, must continue to grow or too soon loses its freshness and potential.

• **Bloom where you are planted.** You don't have to be a better teacher than someone else. You don't have to make more money than someone who went into another field of work. And you don't have to have achieved all the top honors in school or have been acclaimed as the most gorgeous or talented. What you must do is be the best you that you can be. I realize that sounds trite. Yet, how many minds are needlessly stressed, and how much secret self-pain is unnecessarily inflicted because people compare their weaknesses to other peoples' strengths? To agonize or feel jealous that you "should" be more or different than your personal best is to throw away your happiness.

There is a marvelous early 19th century Hasidic tale about a rabbi by the name of Zusya from Hanipol. When he was a young man, he got the idea that the only way he could be a truly good and holy man was to find a perfect person and live as that person would live. He chose Moses. With great devotion, he worked to imitate his ideal. After many years of frustrated effort, Zusya became bitterly disillusioned with the realization that he could never be the person that Moses was. Then one night, he had a powerful dream in which God spoke to him: "My son, Zusya, when you come before my throne I will not ask why you were not Moses. I will ask why you were not Zusya." Every great teacher that I have known has lived the secret of happiness: Bloom where you are planted.

• **Flowers are simply fascinating.** And so is everything else! People talk a great deal about motivation. How do you get students motivated? How does the teacher stay motivated? Well, let's settle these questions right here. I am now going to give you the answer to all of your motivational challenges—in three words—*motivation is fascination*. When a student gets fascinated by the work at hand, that work gets done. When a teacher gets fascinated by the students at hand, those students learn. Fascination is the most powerfully motivating word in the English language. You cannot be bored when you are fascinated. Finding fault with a person you see as fascinating is difficult. How in the world can you be cynical and negative when fascination has you in tow? Fascination is not something that happens to you by accident. It is a decision you choose to make about how you will look at life. Are you married? The most loving decision you will ever make about the future of your marriage is to choose to stay forever fascinated by your beloved. Do you see the same people every day? Get intrigued by everything possible about each of those people. How are they so smart about some things and so dumb about other things? How can they care so much about what other people think and yet care so little? How is it possible to be so beautiful and ugly at the same time? In other words, get fascinated by the fact that you live, work with, and teach real live human beings instead of automatons. Human beings may be frustrating, but they are also fascinating. They certainly add spice to your life.

• **Be a perennial, not an annual.** On his 80th birthday, Bob Hope was asked by Bryant Gumbel of NBC's "Today" show if he could give his secret for maintaining such high energy levels and enthusiasm for entertaining "after all these years." Hope's four-word answer should be emblazoned on the minds of every teacher: "I keep doing shows." The greatest energizer in the world is to know that you can and will make a positive difference in another person's life. That knowledge should keep you showing up day after day, year after year.

• **Keep your roots deep.** Self-communication helps you learn about yourself. It is what you say to yourself in your own private thoughts about yourself and the world around you. Self-communication is the root by which you feed every part of your life. What you allow yourself to believe and therefore to communicate to yourself about your job, town, family, school, students, abilities, capacities for happiness, future, even your looks will be precisely what you will make happen in those areas of your life. Let us say, for example, that for the hundredth time this week, you have heard from the same people the

same excuses for their weak performances. After a while, it gets a bit tedious. You want more from these people, but they simply won't give it. At this point, you have a fundamental, root choice to make: Either you choose to see yourself locked in academic mortal combat with them, or you choose to communicate a different message to yourself (and, by osmosis, to them). That message is, I love teaching challenges; I love teaching you; I love that I feel proud of what I teach. Further, I love feeling good; I will think only those thoughts that keep me feeling good about myself, my life, my profession, and my students. I know that the only way I will ever have any constructive influence is to have such high respect for every person I teach that each individual will see himself or herself reflected in a positive light through my eyes. Sure, some of them are a little unusual, weird even; a few are loud and enjoy being noticed; a couple are perfect, maybe a little too perfect. But everyone needs what I have to give. Come to think of it, these people are pretty fascinating. I might go so far as to say that everyone is beautiful. I could even get biblical about it and say that they are sort of like flowers: "Even Solomon in all his glory was not arrayed like one of these." Of course, when your roots go deeply enough that you are able to talk in this manner to yourself, your life and teaching have reached the stage of an artist, say of William Blake's stature, where you are able

> To see a World in a
> Grain of Sand
> And a Heaven in a
> Wild Flower

Ron Wallen is CEO of Pharmax (a corporate holding company) and President of Performance Success International, a worldwide consulting firm headquartered in San Francisco, California.

More than 30 years ago in an elementary class serving mentally retarded children, some basic truths were learned.

5

More Alike Than Different

BY NORA MARTIN

I knew it was coming. For two weeks, 9-year-old Billie, with his red hair and freckles, had been staring at me day after day. The time finally arrived when he boldly walked up to my desk and asked, "Ms. White [my maiden name], is your mother colored?"

I replied, "Yes, Billie, she is."

Next question, "Is your daddy colored?"

Another answer, "Yes, Billie, he is."

Now the big question, "Is your *whole* family colored?"

My final response, "Yes, my *entire* family is colored."

He walked away from my desk gasping, "Her *whole* family is!"

Later that evening when I shared this experience with my mother, she simply laughed and said, "Why, Nora, he probably thought that your color was a mistake, and being brown could not have happened to an entire family!"

About two months later, Jacky's parents walked into our class unannounced. Both of them took one look at me, smiled, and nodded in agreement with each other. I welcomed them and asked if I could be of service. The father immediately told me that Jacky had been rubbing cocoa on his arms and legs

and sharing with the rest of the family that he wanted to look like his teacher—*me!* We all laughed, and both parents now understood Jacky's reasoning.

Many similar episodes occurred during my first year of teaching (1963-64) in a special education classroom in the Midwest. The students and faculty had limited interaction with "people of color," and I had the unique opportunity of integrating the teaching staff. My arrival prompted a positive article in a large metropolitan newspaper. The article was entitled "Negro Teachers in White Schools."

That year prepared me and my students for some unforgettable human interrelationships. Now, as a seasoned college professor, I find myself reflecting often on that first school year, especially when I conduct workshops or discuss such topics as appreciating diversity or multiculturalism. Billie, Jacky, and their classmates were sincere in their efforts to know what made us different. In honest ways, my responses always focused on our likenesses, realizing that, yes, we *were* different, but we were more *alike* than different. Because these elementary school students were labeled as "educable mentally retarded," we emphasized that a difference is not necessarily a deficit.

During the early 1960s, the United States was experiencing a racial revolution, and there I was, with 15 students, sensibly and honestly discussing racial relations. And only in the last few years has our nation challenged the melting pot theory, yet I can vividly recall that in March 1964, our class had already decided that the United States was really a "salad" and not a combined "stew." We always spoke with pride when we discussed how each part of the salad can be identified and still contribute to the combined dish. We were definitely ahead of our time.

We learned together, played together, and shared our educational lives together. The mean age of those students is now 40 to 43, and I am proud to say that many of us have remained in touch. Last summer, in fact, one young man from that class arrived at my university, gave me a bear hug, and told me about his job and life.

When I hear of current cultural, racial, ethnic, gender, or religious hatred and unrest, I wish that we could have bottled the love and respect we had for each other in that school year more than 30 years ago. Those real, positive feelings have remained.

I think I can speak for that unforgettable class when I say each of them agrees that we would have fewer racial and ethnic problems if we would just simply remember that we are more alike than different.

Nora Martin is a Professor of Special Education at Eastern Michigan University. Martin's warmth, insight, and wit cause her to be in great demand as a motivational speaker and consultant for local school districts and parent organizations. Her specialty areas include mental retardation, learning disabilities, and children prenatally exposed to drugs and alcohol. Martin has also presented numerous speeches and seminars on topics ranging from ways to motivate reluctant learners, to stress reduction for educators, to learning styles.

Joy doesn't always bring laughter, and laughter doesn't always bring joy.

But more often than not, laughter removes some of the joy constrictors in our

lives.

6

Memories of Elementary Laughter

BY STEVE WILSON

I flashed on two memories of my early school days, when an elementary school teacher at an inservice training session asked, "What should I do when all the kids in my class are cracking up with laughter and it's getting to be too much? I'm afraid they will get out of control and won't be able to concentrate on their lessons." The other teachers in the group nodded in understanding. The looks on their faces told me they were all familiar with that kind of giggling, cackling, and irrepressible outburst. I had participated in scenes like that when I was in elementary school, and I wondered if they had, too.

The first memory this question evoked regarded a teacher who tried to limit laughter and got more laughter as a result. When I was in 3rd grade, I was president of my class. One of my duties was to take the daily attendance, row by row, and call aloud the absences to Mrs. Marcowitz, who would record them in her black book. Then I read to the class the announcements, hot from the

Teaching & Joy

mimeo machine in the principal's office. Invariably, Jay, the class clown, would be cutting up somehow, making me laugh and giggle my way through my tasks.

One morning became more giggly than usual, and Mrs. Marcowitz angrily rose up from her desk. She ordered the laughing to halt. Then she ordered Jay to get under the kneehole of her desk (one of her favorite punishments) and stay there while she finished her desk work and he had learned his lesson. We were properly terrified and silent. But not for long.

Jay was humiliated by her treatment and definitely did not like being put under her desk. He had not been there more than three minutes when Mrs. Marcowitz yelped, leapt up from her chair, and hopped around the room in pain. Jay had shown his displeasure by biting her hard on the ankle. I know we all laughed even more hysterically at her. I can't remember what happened after that, but Jay and I still laugh about the wild scene in 3rd grade.

In 5th grade, I experienced a different version of high comedy and hysterical silliness, with a different reaction from the teacher. While attending the William Cullen Bryant Elementary School, a friend and I wrote several humorous skits that our teacher allowed—even encouraged—us to perform in front of the class. But, during one performance, we just couldn't keep a straight face. We cracked each other up, choking on our own laughter so much that we could barely get the words out. I remember hearing my own high-pitched cackling, the kind that drove my mother up the wall, but I could not stop. Tears streaming down our cheeks, sides aching, Jay and I were unable to read from the scripts we had scribbled on lined tablet paper the night before. All of our classmates were breaking up with laughter, and it escalated rapidly.

I have no idea what we thought was so funny, probably because what really mattered at the time was just having fun and impressing the other kids. But something magical happened that day, which has taken me years to understand. Now I know it as an important part of the psychology of mixing work and play.

There, in my 5th grade classroom, doubled over with joyous laughter, I became completely caught up in the joy of the moment and was lost in the euphoriant effect of laughter. I was so "high" that for some moments I was not

aware of anyone or anything other than my own sheer delight. My laughter seemed to be coming from someplace far away as I became lost in a blissful rush of innocence and endorphins. All too soon the scene became quiet, everything snapped back into focus, and we finished the skit. I had definitely lost control, but my teacher had not stopped me from laughing.

Steve Wilson, psychologist and "the Joyologist," is an author, humor educator, and professional speaker, specializing in enjoying life and creating positive working environments in business, health care, and educational organizations. He is in private practice in Columbus, Ohio, and the author of Eat Dessert First, Super Humor Power, The Art of Mixing Work and Play, *and* Remarried with Children.

Miss Daisy filled her 4th grade classroom with wonder, curiosity, and joy.

Before cooperative learning, integrated thematic instruction, problem-solving

curriculums, and recognition of individual differences became well known, she

practiced them all and brought spirit into her teaching.

7

Miss Daisy

BY DONALD DAVIS

In the fourth grade, all the A-through-GRs (still Patricia Abernethy through Thomas Greene, though Leon Connor had gone to Jackson Training School for good by now) ended up in Miss Daisy Rose Boring's class.

Miss Daisy was one of the six daughters of Mr. Robert Boring. Mr. Boring had started Boring's Hardware in 1909, and having no son to take over the business, had hired Daddy to work for him in 1924.

Sixteen years later, Mr. Boring died, and the six sisters sold the store to Daddy, who still ran it as Boring's Hardware. That same year, he married Mother, having waited, properly, until he could adequately support a wife and family.

Instead of entering the hardware business the six daughters had years before become school teachers . . . for life!

Source: From *Listening for the Crack of Dawn* by Donald Davis (August House, 1990). Copyright © 1990 by Donald Davis, Storyteller, Inc. Reprinted by permission.

I had not had Miss Lily, who taught second grade at Sulpher Springs School. She taught the GU-through-M class.

Anyone who had one of the Boring sisters for any grade in school usually spent the next year wondering, "Will I get the next one?" They taught all the even-numbered grades (2, 4, 6, 8, 10, and senior English) at Sulpher Springs School. If your name fell just right in the alphabet, it was possible to receive half of your entire public education from the Boring sisters.

Mr. Robert, their father (we never heard anything about their mother), tried to give all of them botanical names. He did well through Miss Lily, Miss Pansy and Miss Violet. He must have thought Miss Daisy Rose would be the last, for he used two flowers in naming her. (Perhaps he was convinced a boy would come next.) When two more girls appeared, he started on gemstones. The youngest were Miss Opal and Miss Pearl.

Miss Daisy had taught fourth grade for forty-one years. She was a tiny, frail-looking woman in her early sixties. Her bird-like appearance prompted all of us to begin our first day of school wondering whether that little old woman could really handle us. We had, after all, been at this for three years already. The A-through- GRs were a tough bunch!

As we were whispering and wondering, Miss Daisy was giving what she called "housekeeping" instructions to the class. This consisted of instructions on everything from how to use the pencil sharpener to where to hang your coat.

The door of the classroom was standing open to the hall, and a mouse, who had had the entire school to himself all summer and was now trying inno-cently to escape this first-day invasion of wild children, came into our room in search of a safe place of retreat.

The mouse, scared to death, made its way a few cautious steps and sniffs at a time along the base of the blackboard wall just behind Miss Daisy.

No one was watching Miss Daisy. Every eye in the classroom was on the mouse. All of us secretly knew that very soon Miss Daisy would realize that we were not watching her. "This will be the test," I thought. "As soon as she turns to see what we're watching, we'll see what she's made of!"

Teaching & Joy

In a few moments Miss Daisy caught on. She turned to see what we were staring at, and spotted the brown mouse just as it reached the corner of the room. She didn't make a sound.

Very quietly she opened the side drawer of her desk and took out two brown paper towels. We all watched, rapt, as the tiny woman slipped quietly toward the corner where the mouse was, squatted slowly to the floor, reached out, and caught the mouse in the brown paper towels.

She carried the mouse back to her desk (still in the towels), held it up in front of us. With one hand—*crrrunch*—crushed it to death and dropped it in the trash can!

Not a sound came from anyone in the room. ("Quiet as a mouse," I thought later.) After that, no one ever had any doubts about Miss Daisy's power; we listened to every word she said.

The whole course of the year was going to be great fun. As she described her plan to us, Miss Daisy was going to take us, without our ever leaving our room at Sulpher Springs School, on an imaginary trip around the world.

It was going to be a year of play. Each day we'd get out our maps and plan our travels. Then, with Miss Daisy's help, we'd go on our travels for the day.

She didn't pass out the spelling books. She didn't even pass out the arithmetic books. We were just going to play all year.

Our imaginary plan was this: we would get some of our parents to pretend to drive us to Atlanta in their cars. I was not sure about whether Daddy would take the blue Dodge. He didn't usually like to travel very far from home.

Once in Atlanta, our plan was to board the train. Miss Daisy told us all about it. It was "the wonderful Southern Crescent," with a dining car that had fresh-cut flowers and real sterling silver on the tables. We were all to ride the train to New Orleans.

After a day or two in New Orleans, we would load up on what Miss Daisy called a "tramp steamer," and steam away for South America.

The real truth was that Miss Daisy had never actually been out of Nantahala County in her life except for four brief years some forty-one years in the past when she had ridden the train less than a hundred miles to Asheville

Normal to learn to teach fourth grade. But for forty-one years she had sent away by mail and had ordered thousands and thousands and thousands of picture postcards. It was not possible for us to go anywhere on our imaginary travels, from a small town in Alabama to a temple garden in Japan, without Miss Daisy being able to dig down through her files of shoe-boxes to finally come up with a postcard to show us what that place looked like.

Some of the cards were very old, with black-and-white pictures and ragged edges. We were fascinated by the old ones most of all.

As we went on our travels, we had to write down the names of all the places we visited and the things we saw: states, towns, geographical and historical sites, even crops and industries. We made long lists of famous people who had lived everywhere we went. We learned about all the things they had done.

All year long we worked at this without ever figuring out that Miss Daisy had us making up our own lists of spelling words. They were words which were much harder than those in the slender fourth-grade spelling books she had never bothered to pass out.

We also never figured out (or was it because we didn't want to admit it) that as we calculated how far we had traveled each day, how much money we spent for gasoline or food or tickets, how to change money from one country to another, and how to calculate latitude and longitude, we were doing arithmetic. Miss Daisy never called it that. We were just doing what you have to do to make your way around the world.

The class was divided into four "travel teams." Most of each morning was spent in planning each day's travels. Each team was given certain parts of the journey to take the class on. Miss Daisy would flit from team to team as we planned. She was informer, guide, questioner, always insisting that no matter how much we learned, she could always learn more in a day than we could!

Each afternoon, on a strictly alternating schedule, two of the four "travel teams" would take the class on their assigned part of the journey.

Miss Daisy explained it this way: "It takes twice as long to plan anything as it does to do it, so you get two days to plan before you present. 'Plan-plan-present, plan-plan-present,' that's the pattern we work on."

She called the first day of planning "rounding up" and the second day "closing in on it."

On Fridays Miss Daisy did all the presenting herself, filling in our gaps and giving us what felt like a day off. This did help to make up for the tests, which also always came on Fridays.

We worked our way to Atlanta, then on to New Orleans, where we finally boarded a steamer named the "Aurelia" for our trip to South America.

The first day of sailing was very rough! One of the "travel teams" was charged with teaching us all about the ship we were sailing on. They decided it would be a good idea to list all the parts of the ship, and learning to spell those awful words with their apostrophes and unpronounced extra letters nearly made some of us seasick.

On Friday of that week we came to school very excited, wondering what Miss Daisy might have in store for us on her day to present. As we gathered in the room a boy named Lucius Grasty, one of the last of the GRs, came running into the room.

His head was stooped and he wore a wool knit toboggan. The home-made hat was pulled way down over his ears. He wouldn't take it off though it was still September, and not even beginning to get cold yet.

Lucius went straight to the back of the room, squatted in a corner, and refused to come out.

Miss Daisy came breezing into the room, took little notice of Lucius, and began the day.

"Today, children," she started in a hurry, "we cross the equator!"

"That was fast," I thought.

"Have any of you ever crossed the equator?" she asked. We met the question with blank stares. We didn't even understand what she was talking about.

"Good," she went on, "because when we cross the equator we must have a big party for Neptune, King of the Deep."

As she kept talking about King Neptune, she went back into the cloak closet and started bringing out things that had been left there by kids at the end of school for forty-one years. Out she came with old coats, abandoned

caps and hats, odd galoshes, umbrellas with broken ribs, even brooms and mops.

"On a ship, we have to work with what we have," she said as she began to dress us up for the party. Mop-heads became wigs and we took off our shoes and socks like sailors. She pulled the shades way out from the windows and twisted them at an angle to make sails for the ship. We found a rope and took turns throwing one another overboard out the first floor window, and pulling each other back onto the ship again. She came up with a shaving mug from somewhere, lathered the boys up, and shaved them with a sword made from a yardstick.

"Some sailors even have their clothes run up the mast," she said. No one volunteered for that one!

"And some," she said, as she eased back through the room to where Lucius was still squatting on the floor (he had taken part in nothing), ". . . some *special* sailors, like the captain's son on his first voyage, even have their heads shaved!"

As she spoke those words, she lifted Lucius's toboggan. There we saw it: he was the sailor whose head was shaved! We were all jealous. How did *Lucius* get to be the special one?

It was a long time later that I overheard Mother telling a friend about that day and learned that when Lucius had gone home the day before, his mother had found lice in his hair. She had shaved his head and washed it in kerosene to get rid of the lice. Miss Daisy had taken that little boy with the blistered head, and in a moment had transformed him into the hero of crossing the equator.

At last we made land in South America. After leaving the steamer, we visited our first city, Belim, where we discovered that everyone spoke not Spanish but Portuguese. Then we hired small boats and guides to take us up the Amazon River.

Miss Daisy would stand in front of the classroom and say, "The Amazon is the longest river in the Americas. There are giant ferns there, ferns as big as trees. And butterflies—there are butterflies so big you could ride them . . . if you could catch one!"

Some of us who thought we were pretty smart would try to argue with her about the "longest river" idea. We would gather the maps and say, "Miss Daisy, what about the Mississippi and the Missouri put together? That's really just one river. They just got two names on it a long time ago. If you put all of it together, it's longer than the Amazon, isn't it?"

"Two names, two rivers," she replied. "The Amazon is the longest. Remember that—it will be on the test!"

No matter where we went after that (all the way down to the tip of South America, on an imaginary ice-breaker to the South Pole, up the Congo, and down the Nile), the Amazon was always my favorite place.

That was because my big art project for the year was making a butterfly "so big you could ride on it."

Several months earlier my Uncle Floyd had tried to invent a flying machine. He had made a two-part framework out of copper tubing and the flat sides of orange crates. It was joined in the middle by a long piano hinge so that the wings could flap.

Once the basic construction was finished, he had glued what looked like two million white-leghorn feathers to both sides of the "wings." Finally he rigged a harness to the underside so that the wings could be strapped on his back and he could flap them with his arms.

When the glue was all dry, he carried the huge wings up a ladder to the roof of the front porch of his house.

He told us all about it later. "I was going to try a little test flight from the house out to that red maple tree," he said, "but a downdraft got me!"

He sprained his ankle crash-landing. He was lucky he hadn't broken his neck.

The lucky thing for *me* was that the crash didn't tear up the wings. As soon as the Friday after the art project assignments came, I started begging Daddy to take me to Uncle Floyd's. Once there, I started begging Uncle Floyd for the wings.

After taking off the harness straps to be sure that I couldn't try to fly with them, he gave me the wings for the foundation of my butterfly. We folded them by the piano hinge and took them home in the blue Dodge.

I went to work. The body was made out of some big mailing tubes with the ends stopped up. The head was a rubber ball, with pieces of coat hanger bent to the shape of antennae.

The big job was painting the wings. It took nearly all day Saturday. Yellow and green, blue and red, purple and orange, swirls and patterns, matching on both sides of both wings, until by the end of the day I had created a butterfly so big you could really ride on it.

The only problem was that with the body and all the paint I had used, the wings wouldn't flap by the piano hinge anymore. It took all day Sunday for the paint to dry.

On Monday morning Daddy said he would take Joe-brother and me to school in the blue Dodge. "I don't think that thing will go through the door of the school bus," was his excuse.

Now that the paint was dry and the wings were stiff, it wouldn't fit through the door of the Dodge either. So Daddy drove us to school very slowly, with the window rolled down, holding the big butterfly outside the window. Several times he pulled to the side of the road to let the cars pass which had backed up behind us as he drove slowly enough to keep the butterfly from taking off.

When I got to the classroom with the butterfly, Miss Daisy was thrilled! She fastened a wire to the butterfly's back, climbed on top of a desk in the middle of the room, and suspended the butterfly from one of the light fixtures.

For the remainder of the year it hung there, multicolored and beautiful, decorating the room and reminding us of the Amazon.

We traveled overland from the headwaters of the Amazon to the very tip of Cape Horn, took an icebreaker for a brief visit to a scientific research station on "that frozen, southernmost continent," then sailed to Cape Good Hope and up the west coast of Africa to the mouth of the Congo.

Teaching & Joy

We hired small boats and guides to travel up the Congo. Miss Daisy showed us a postcard picture of logs being burned out to build dug-out canoes, and we were sure they were ours.

To our surprise, the Congo was not like the Amazon at all. Here we met shining black tribes ranging from Pygmies to Zulus, and we saw sharp-nosed crocodiles instead of alligators.

At the head of the Congo, we joined a safari which took us by Jeep and then on foot all the way to Victoria Falls, and on to the very beginning waters of the Nile.

As soon as the Nile was navigable, we built huge rafts, supplied them, and floated for days and days until we landed at last beside the pyramids.

After a short time of sailing on the Mediterranean, we landed for a visit to the brand-new country of Israel. It could have been an old country as far as our visit was concerned, because all the things we visited were, in Miss Daisy's words, "nearly two thousand important years old."

If the United States Supreme Court (the "Nine Old Men in Washington," Uncle Floyd called them) ever happened to come down to Sulpher Springs School to be sure that the separation of church and state was being properly maintained, they would have found Miss Daisy dutifully teaching us to spell the names of the leaders of the new nation of Israel, and other important fourth-grade facts such as the distance from Jerusalem to Cairo.

They never came, though, and so when school let out for Christmas holidays, Miss Daisy told us we could stay over in Bethlehem while school was out. In spite of what the Supreme Court may or may not have seen had they been there, none of us was at all uncertain about why it was important to her that we go home for Christmas thinking of Bethlehem.

After Christmas, we again set sail on the Mediterranean, this time bound for Greece and then on to Europe.

While we were in Greece, one of the four "travel teams" was assigned to take us to the ancient Olympic games. This group decided that we really should have Olympic games of our own. Miss Daisy thought the idea was great.

"There is only one thing I must warn you about, boys and girls. In the old Olympic games the athletes competed with no clothes on." We all looked around the room and stared at one another.

Miss Daisy went on. "But since it's wintertime, I suppose we will have to wear clothing for our Olympics. Does anyone mind that?" It was as quiet in the room as when the mouse died.

On Friday (no tests this week) we all came to school with sheets to wrap over our clothes. It looked more like a ninth-grade Latin banquet than the Olympics, but we didn't care. Miss Daisy had even made laurel wreaths for the winners.

It was a day of great competition. Relays were run back and forth from one end of the playground to another, passing a baton made from an empty paper-towel roller.

There was shot-put with wooden croquet balls, javelin throwing with sharp wooden tobacco sticks, and finally a marathon which went from the school yard out and all the way down Railroad Street, around a big oak tree at the post office, back behind the stores on Main Street, ending at a finish line on the school ground just across the creek from where we had begun.

Running wrapped in a sheet was going to be difficult. We did as well as we could to tie the sheets up between the legs of our blue jeans so we could move more freely.

I wasn't much of a competitor in either the shot-put or the javelin contests. Not being able to throw straight made it all but impossible to figure out just how far you could throw when a straight line was the object. Pauletta Donaldson won both these contests, but then she was the biggest kid in the fourth grade, boy or girl, and had longer arms than all the rest of us.

The relays were more even. Our team of four came in in second place and could have won if the baton hadn't been dropped twice (the winning team only dropped theirs once). At the very end of the day came the marathon.

The fastest down-and-out runner in the class was a tiny boy named Hallie Curtis. Everyone was pretty sure that Hallie could take the marathon with no competition.

Hallie was very small and had two cow-licks in his hair. One was over his right eye and the other near the crown of his head. His hair insisted on standing up in these two places, and Hallie couldn't stand it. It was hard enough being teased about being little. The cow-licks were too much.

Hallie would put lard on his hair in a futile attempt to make the wild spots lie down. It never worked for very long. The lard, however, vulnerable as it was to Hallie's body temperature, gradually ran down his face and neck. His shirt collar was always dark and greasy with melted hair-lard.

Hallie had the longest arms for his body of anyone we had ever seen. His hands seemed to dangle alongside his knees as he walked along. Hallie's special trick was that he could bend just a bit and run on all fours, just like a greyhound or a whippet—though he looked more like a greasy, escaped, dressed-up baboon. It was simply true: Hallie Curtis, running on all four legs, could completely outrun any boy or girl in any grade at Sulpher Springs School.

Before the marathon started, everyone complained to Miss Daisy that Hallie's four-legged running was not fair. So, to be fair, Miss Daisy warned him, "Now, Hallie, no running on your hands. You have to run on two feet like everybody else does. Those old Greeks didn't run on four legs!"

Miss Daisy lined us up. "One for the money, two for the show, three to get ready, and four . . . to . . . GO!"

Off we went, sheets flapping, girls screaming, across the playground, then spread out a little now, through the schoolyard gate and down the side of the empty street which ran behind Main Street and along by the railroad tracks.

The first half of the race told nothing. The sprinters rushed ahead, then started to wear out as the whole column began the mid-point turn around the oak tree at the post office.

On the way back the race really settled down. There was one good solid group of runners in the middle, with a slowly growing assortment of stragglers stringing out behind.

Out in front of everybody else, the real race was between Hallie Curtis and Pauletta Donaldson. She was nearly a foot taller and ran with flailing arms and

long, gangling paces. Hallie's little legs seemed to spin like eggbeaters. His individual short strides couldn't even be seen as separate steps at all.

When they entered the gate to the school-yard and poured on the heat for the finish line, Pauletta began to pull farther and farther ahead.

Hallie couldn't stand the thought of losing to a girl. He didn't care if Miss Daisy had said that he had to run on two legs. He dropped to all-fours, and looking like a greasy-headed dog wrapped in a sheet, began to close the gap as the two of them outran everyone else toward the finish line.

A little creek ran down the middle of the schoolyard and the finish line was across this little creek from where we were coming back onto the playground from the post office. The last thing all the runners had to do before crossing the finish line was to jump the creek.

It wasn't a hard creek to jump. We jumped it every day during recess as a regular part of most games, but I had never seen Hallie jump it while running on all fours like a dog.

As Hallie and Pauletta approached the creek, Hallie took the lead. He was nearly twenty feet ahead of her when, with a great push of his hind legs, he took to the air, arms reaching out in front of him, then coming back to touch the ground as his legs moved forward for the next step.

Something happened. Hallie's legs seemed to tangle in midair so that he couldn't pull his knees up. Instead of sailing across the creek, he fell like a rock, flat on his belly, in the middle of the water.

Pauletta never missed a step. She jumped right across him, and with a look of certain pride on her face, crossed the finish line alone.

Later we learned what had happened. Hallie's nose was itching as he came across the playground field on all fours. He tried to hold back a sneeze as long as he could, but just as he started to leave the ground for his great leap across the creek, the long-saved-up sneeze burst loose. The great escape of the held-back sneeze snapped Hallie's belt right in two, and his blue jeans fell down to his knees, where they tangled hopelessly with the sheet which was tied up between his knees.

The sheet did protect his modesty, but the tangle had brought him down in great agony of defeat. He had lost to a girl.

Pauletta was simply disgusting as she wore her laurel wreath for the rest of the entire day.

When we finished with Greece, we made a great circle through Europe and spent the rest of the springtime crossing Asia: China, Japan, down to New Zealand and Australia, then over the Pacific, past Pearl Harbor and on to Los Angeles.

The last month of the school year was a long imaginary train ride, not across the United States, but across *North America*, Canada to Mexico, until on the last day of May, there we were, right back in our classroom at Sulpher Springs School.

The next year the A-through-GRs got Mrs. Kinney for the fifth grade. Mother said Mrs. Kinney was very smart, that we were lucky to have her, but it seemed like a long year as she tried to teach us how interesting the Greeks and Romans were, straight out of the book.

I had none of Miss Daisy's sisters in later years, and gradually I forgot about her as the importance of growing up made the fourth grade unreal, unimportant, and further and further behind.

At least ten years passed. I had graduated from Sulpher Springs High School and been away from home and college for a couple of years when I came home to work for the summer.

My job for this particular summer was working as bus boy in the dining room of the Mountain Vale Inn. The Mountain Vale Inn was an old hotel which topped the hill above "Old Main Street." It was the kind of place where retired Floridians spent the entire summer, while residents of Sulpher Springs had still not learned to charge them Florida prices.

It was a place with a dining room, a place where local residents went out for evening meals and after church on Sunday.

We served supper each evening from five until eight o'clock.

One afternoon about four-thirty, I was outside sweeping off the steps and the sidewalk to the dining room when an old two-tone brown LaSalle sedan pulled up into the parking side of the yard.

Though I had not seen it in years, I knew the ancient car well. With its double-spares on the back and its landau trim, there was not another car like it anywhere in Nantahala County.

The LaSalle belonged to the Boring sisters. It had been their father's last car, new when he died, and they had carefully kept it. More than twenty years later, they were still keeping it—and driving it, it seemed, all over Nantahala County.

Miss Lily was driving that day. She opened her door and got out. As she walked around the long nose of the LaSalle, the other front door opened, and Miss Opal got out. The two of them opened the back door, lifted something from the back seat, and began to walk side by side up the sidewalk to the dining room.

I looked more closely and saw that they had between them all that was left of my old Miss Daisy.

A tiny skin-and-bones figure, less than half, it seemed, of the tiny thing she had been more than a decade earlier when I was in the fourth grade. She was between them, with each holding an arm as they brought her up the walk, little toes barely touching the ground. They were taking her out to supper.

As soon as I recognized them, I hurried down the walk to meet them. Miss Lily recognized me at once and spoke to me. Then she turned to Miss Daisy and said, "Look, Daisy. Look! It's one of your little boys . . . all grown up."

Miss Daisy lifted her head and it did turn toward me, but her eyes were colorless and blank and empty. Nobody in there. After a long moment, her head dropped back to her chest.

My curiosity asked for a response. It came from Miss Lily. "Daisy has had a stroke," she offered.

While I was thinking that perhaps they were pushing things a bit having her out too soon in this condition I asked, "When did she have it?"

In unison they replied, "She's had it six years." Miss Lily continued, "She got it when she retired."

I stood aside and watched as they partly led, partly carried, Miss Daisy up the steps and into the dining room for her supper.

Once inside, I tried to do my work without staring, but from time to time did glance to see Miss Lily and Miss Opal cutting up tiny bites on Miss Daisy's plate. They mashed green beans and bits of potato, then helped her swallow it with drinks from a small glass of milk.

Part of my job was to clear the dishes from tables as soon as people were finished with their meals so that the dessert tray could be brought to the table.

It looked like they were finished, so I rolled my dish cart to their table and began clearing things away as quickly as I could.

Suddenly, in the midst of my doing this job, I was paralyzed by the strange feeling of someone staring at me. I looked toward the feeling, and it was Miss Daisy.

She was staring straight at me, and her eyes were sparkling and clear. They were alive, and as blue as they had ever been.

Her lips began to quiver and then move as from somewhere way down inside of her tiny body a thin, wispy ghost-of-a-voice came to life and softly said, straight to me, "The Amazon is the longest . . . there are butterflies here we can ride on . . . "

Then her eyes went blank and her head dropped back to her chest.

I grabbed my dish cart and ran for the kitchen.

Mr. Gibbons, the old cook, was looking out of the kitchen door and muttering to himself, "Isn't it sad about poor Miss Daisy . . . isn't it sad."

"No, it's not!" I thought, but only to myself. "No, it's not sad." Until a few moments ago I had thought the same thing, but now I felt as if I had made the greatest discovery in the world and had to find some way to explain it to Mr. Gibbons.

Then I remembered. "Mr. Gibbons," I said, "way back in Miss Daisy's room in the fourth grade sometimes we would get so full of learning new things and so tired of that traveling that we would look at her and say, 'Miss Daisy, why do

we have to learn all these things?'" In memory, I could still see Miss Daisy holding her mouse-crushing fist high in the air, clenched, as she answered the question.

"She would say, 'Because, boys and girls . . . *because!* One of these days, when you grow up, you'll be able to go anywhere you want to. When that day comes, you simply must know where you are going!'

"You see, it's not sad, Mr. Gibbons," I pleaded, returning to the present, "because I have seen that Miss Daisy is in a world in which she can go anywhere she wants to go, and she knows where she's going. Why, she can even ride the butterflies."

We looked back into the dining room, but they had finished and were gone. We heard the LaSalle whining from the driveway. I never saw Miss Daisy again.

Donald Davis was born in a southern Appalachian mountain rich in stories. Uncle Frank, a man who "talked in stories," helped Donald capture the real and daily adventure of life, and Davis credits Uncle Frank with giving him the creative courage to tell the stories.

As a student at Davidson College, a graduate of Duke University Divinity School, and a retired Methodist minister, Davis has broadened and enriched his storytelling repertory. He has served as Chairman of the Board of Directors for the National Association for the Preservation and Perpetuation of Storytelling and performed as a featured storyteller at the Smithsonian Institution, at the World's Fair, and on the National Public Radio program "Good Evening."

Davis has produced numerous award-winning sound recordings and published seven books, including story collections, an instructional book on story creation, a novel, and a children's picture book.

Recent reports that common sense is dead have been greatly exaggerated.

Like other great educators, Jim Fay helps to keep common sense alive.

8

How to Give Your Kids an Unfair Advantage

BY JIM FAY

Susie came from Asia as an adopted child. She joined a family with solid values of achievement and personal responsibility. In a few short years, Susie had moved to the head of her class. Her classmates periodically asked her about why she got high grades. They thought Asians usually excelled at academics, but Susie said that she always did her homework before she went out to play.

Susie became valedictorian of her high school class. This achievement caught the attention of many parents of the other children. "Why is this?" they asked. "She lives in an Anglo family, but performs like an Asian." One couple actually called Susie's parents for the answer. Susie's father mentioned that they shared some of the Asian values of hard work, struggle, and personal responsibility. He said Susie was expected to be responsible and when she was not, natural consequences were applied. He also mentioned that he and his wife expected Susie to do her chores, be respectful of her parents, and apply herself to her schoolwork.

"Susie knows where we stand," said Dad. "She knows that in the United States she has the right to life, liberty, and the pursuit of happiness—not the right to life, liberty, and someone else to provide happiness for her. Susie is busy pursuing her own happiness through achievement and personal responsibility."

"Wait a minute!" replied the other parents. "Doesn't that give her an unfair advantage over the other children? This is the United States; whatever became of equal opportunity?"

"I guess if you look at it that way, there may never be equal opportunity," Susie's father responded. "As long as some people work harder than others and place a high value upon achievement through struggle, they will always have an advantage. I guess that's the United States I know."

The Value of Struggle

Every time we hire new employees at Cline/Fay Institute, we don't look at their school grades; instead, we interview intensely to determine their level of personal responsibility. Can they get up on time and arrive at work on time? Do they take responsibility for their own actions? Are they positive people who pursue their own success, or do they wait for others to hand it to them? Do they blame the system or others for their problems?

The founding fathers of the United States dedicated our nation to life, liberty, and the pursuit of happiness. Our citizens had a chance for success through struggle, and as a result, struggle made the United States great. Over the years, we have gradually moved toward an attitude of protecting our children from struggle. Many parents say, "I don't want my children to have to struggle like I did. I want them to have a better life and all the things I never had."

We see the results of this attitude in our public schools. Fewer and fewer children appear willing to accept struggle as a necessary part of learning. Teachers work hard to find ways to motivate students, and students believe

teachers are mean when they ask students to struggle. Schools are criticized because students do not achieve as well as in the past. Until our entire society changes its message about the value of struggle, however, the United States will be plagued with underachieving students. That's the bad news.

The good news is that your child can stand out and have a real advantage over the others. Children who learn to struggle early in life have the advantage. They also learn to be responsible. When teachers ask them to struggle to achieve, these kids think, "No big deal, I get what I want through struggle."

Giving Your Child the Advantage

Parents can give their children an "unfair advantage" in a number of ways. Here are a few of them. I promise, if you practice using them, you will be pleasantly surprised with your success.

Chores

Learn to get your children to do their chores without a battle. Regardless of what your kids say about chores being unfair or that none of their friends have to do chores, children need to contribute to the welfare of the family. Children as young as 6 can do a minimum of 20 minutes of chores each day.

List all the jobs necessary for your family to survive. Keep the list on the refrigerator, and add new ones as you think of them. This list includes all the jobs the parents usually do, such as earning the money, keeping the checkbook, paying the bills, driving the car, shopping, cooking, making beds, and washing clothes. Invite the children to list the things they need their parents to do for them.

Hold a family meeting to divide up the jobs. Ask the children to select the jobs they think they would most like to do. If they don't like any of the jobs, have them choose the ones that they hate the least. Be careful not to assign jobs that require children to depend upon each other. Such chores just lead to arguments.

One technique for getting chores done is to say, "There is no hurry each day to do the jobs. Just be sure they are done before the end of the day." Do not remind them about the chores. If the jobs are not completed by the end of the day, say nothing and let the children go to bed. Let them sleep for 30 to 45 minutes and then wake them up, reminding them that the end of the day is near and that they are to get up and finish their work. Don't take "no" for an answer.

Matching Funds

Children are bombarded with media advertisements about their needs for material things. Parents may be tempted to give all they can as a show of love. Yet, this unconditional giving robs children of the opportunity to struggle and puts them at risk for underachievement in school.

Parents may also be tempted to say, "You don't need those things." This type of answer is ineffective. Even in the rare event that a parent can convince a child, such an attitude robs the child of a chance to struggle. The times when children ask you to buy them something are opportunities to provide success through struggle—the time for the parent to implement "matching funds."

Tommy announces, "I really need those basketball shoes. All the other children have them and they're only $120."

The wise parent responds with, "You ought to have them. I can't wait to see how you look in them. I'll contribute $60. As soon as you earn the rest, you'll have those shoes."

"But, it's not fair. The other children's parents buy them."

"I know. It's rough living the way we do. Let me know when you're ready for the $60."

Tommy will wear those new shoes with greater pride once *he* has struggled to earn them. Children who earn what they get learn self-respect, resourcefulness, the value of money, and most important, that problems are solved through struggle.

Your value system dictates the amount you provide each time. Sometimes you contribute 75 percent, sometimes 10 percent, and sometimes even 90 percent. No firm rule applies. It's your money. You get to decide. And remember that a gift once in a while doesn't hurt a thing.

Offering More Than One Solution

Children who solve their own problems have more self-respect than those who don't. As adults, we are tempted to run interference for children because, as adults, we find it hard to see children having problems. However, parents who frequently solve their children's problems raise children who are emotionally crippled. These children come to believe the parents' unstated message that children can't solve their own problems.

Many children "drop the ball" when they have a problem. They look to their parents with pathetic voices: "I can't do it."

And many parents say, "Oh no. If I don't pick up the ball, the child will never do it for himself." These parents soon find themselves sucked into their child's problem. The sad part is that most parents will tell you that their children never seem to like the parents' solutions anyway.

The next time your child comes to you with a problem, listen with empathy and follow with a question: "It sounds like that's really bothering you. What do you think you're going to do?"

Most children will say, "I don't know."

Then you can say, "That's sad not to know. Would you like to hear what some other children have tried?"

If the youngster says, "Yes," tell the child you will give it some thought and respond later. You will have a chance to think it out or to call a friend to help you make up a list of good and bad suggestions.

The important point here is to provide some choices for the child instead of just one solution. Present these solutions to the child one at a time, and at the same time, require the child to evaluate the solution. For example, "Some children get an army of their friends together and threaten the kid who is calling them names. How do you think that would work out?"

I watched a parent use this approach once. In this case, she couldn't think of a good solution, so she suggested four bad solutions and each time asked, "How would that work?"

Finally the youngster said, "Those ideas aren't any good. I think I'll just go try to talk it out with her." This mother said that seeing her daughter learn to think for herself was great.

Achievement Is Its Own Reward

In talking with children who are not doing well in school, I sometimes ask this question, "Who do you think worries the most about your grades, you or your parents?"

I always get the same answer, "My parents."

As long as children have others who will worry about their problems, they don't have to. They seem to say, "My parents have that worry well in hand. No sense in both of us worrying about it."

Parents who offer money for good grades or punishment for bad grades are taking over too much of the worry about the grades. This attitude also raises the odds that the child will see achievement as something being forced rather than offered. Once a youngster sees grades as part of a power struggle, the issue is no longer the value of a good education, but who is going to win. As long as a child has two choices, to succeed or not to succeed, success still has a good chance. However, a child in a power struggle can only see one choice: winning the power struggle.

Jim Fay is coauthor of Parenting with Love and Logic *and numerous other books, articles, audiocassettes, and videocassettes. "Love and Logic" is a way of working with children that puts parents in control, teaches children to think for themselves, and builds responsible children who are prepared for the real world.*

Fay is a consultant with more than 30 years in the field of education, including work as an elementary school principal. His years in education make him uniquely qualified to help parents learn to run their homes as much like

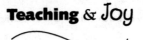
the real world as possible. His approach is based upon three rules: Parents set limits by taking care of themselves; parents provide choices instead of orders whenever possible; parents use natural consequences, with empathy, to do the teaching.

For more information about "Love and Logic," call the Cline/Fay Institute at 1-800-338-4065.

Teaching for Joy

If you were 22 years old and just starting out again, would you choose teaching as a profession? Don't answer until you've read this story.

9

Reflections of Joy

BY VIRGINIA MCCLARY DELATTE

"He's only a teacher," the young visitor in my house casually said of her father.

Only a teacher? She has no idea . . . .

From my earliest realization that I would some day have to earn a living, I knew that I wanted to teach. I taught everything and everyone who would let me: sister, brother, neighboring children, dolls. During World War II, our summer beach home was 15 miles from town. Because driving was limited, I taught Sunday school on our front porch.

One morning, my brother Clebe interrupted me as we were closing a session with sentence prayers. I had thought he was too young to participate, but his shrill, "Hey, wait a minute, 'Ginia. You forgot me!" brought us to a screeching halt. I apologized, and we all waited for his contribution. We had thanked God for almost everything children consider important. Clebe labored, "Fank you, God, for . . . Fank you, God, for . . . ." Just then, our dog bounded up the front steps. "Fank you, God, for Rusty! Amen!"

During my last semester of college, I couldn't wait to begin my practice teaching. "When do *we* start teaching?"

"Can you be ready tomorrow?"

"Yes!"

Thus began the joy of the excitement and preparation so vital to interacting with young minds.

I once had an interview with a principal of a school that was using homogenous grouping. I was asked the question, "What kind of student do you like to teach?"

"One who wants to learn!" was my response then . . . and now. Helping young people toward understanding, creative reasoning, and the challenge of their full potential is a joyful experience.

Since those early teaching days, I have taught kindergarten and 5th through 12th grades. I have also taught in a community college, and one semester, I taught a group of Italian adults to speak English. Joy came to me in those years, often in unexpected ways.

One little girl in my kindergarten class might very well be a teacher today. She reminded me of myself in some ways, but she took charge even more. Later that next year, I substituted for a 1st grade teacher. Before I could even look over the lesson plans, that same little miss, now a take-charge 1st grader, began explaining the routine to me! She had become my colleague, and joy danced between us as student and teacher momentarily changed places.

Nana Dessipris was a Greek kindergartner for whom English was a second language. She was quiet, well behaved, and highly intelligent. I was devastated one day to learn that her father was being reassigned to their homeland and she would be leaving. Soft-spoken, with a beautiful, shy smile, Nana would create a void in my heart and in our classroom. I asked the director to contact Nana's father to come for a conference before he left so I could talk with him about Nana and share some of the insights I had gained. "Oh!" she exclaimed, "He would never come. He is a general!"

"He's a *father*, isn't he? Ask him."

As General Dessipris and I sat in our diminutive chairs and shared our feelings and information about Nana (who must certainly be a successful woman today), I became aware of that illusive joy that only a teacher can experience

when she realizes a beloved student will be well cared for outside the class-room. Her family's love and concern would be the foundation of security for Nana, who would be moved not just from school to school but from country to country during her formative years.

As a teacher for more than 34 years, with teaching experience in Depart-ment of Defense schools in France and Italy, I have had the opportunity to note differences between U.S. teachers and those of almost every other country. Many of my students were children of our NATO allies, mostly Greeks, Turks, and Italians. The Greek students stand out in memory as consistent scholars. Generally, the foreign students were in awe of the U.S. teachers, making it clear they were not used to having a teacher become involved with subjects outside the classroom curriculum. My understanding was that a tremendous distance is maintained between teacher and student, and the twain shall never meet out-side of academics. United States teachers, on the other hand, are frequently known to leap across that distance and risk becoming involved with their stu-dents on an individual basis to create the best possible learning environment for them.

Teaching is not for everyone. Teaching is difficult and often undervalued in dollars and cents. Many teachers supplement inadequate classroom resources with supplies purchased at their own expense. The day-to-day challenges of a classroom in the '90s can be mind-boggling and yet . . . I envy those bright-eyed young teachers just getting started. Joys? Here the monetary aspect pales compared with the intangible, true gold of cherished memories. . . . All good teachers have treasure houses of faces stored in their minds. Some are cap-tured, frozen in time, and we always see them as they were in our classroom. Some we are fortunate enough to watch grow and mature. We may occasion-ally be surprised by how a former student looks today, but we are never sur-prised by their accomplishments. Teachers take quiet but vast pride in today's proud parents, teachers, doctors, actors, scholars, athletes, clerks, and others. Our homes fill to overflowing with notes, cards, trinkets, class photos, and those precious thank you letters—"Your class influenced my career choice. . . ."

Teaching & Joy

Does any other profession in the world allow you to see your work in completion 20 years later, and to see that work express its gratitude for your help in its growth process? That is *JOY*.

Virginia McClary Delatte taught school for more than 30 years. She spent 23 of those years teaching in Europe.

Sometimes we team-teach without another adult in the room. Sometimes we become music teachers when we listen to the songs in the heart of a child.

10

Magic

BY CAROLYN MAMCHUR

I met Eileen in 1976. I had meant to take a sabbatical year in Florida to earn an Ed.D., but had fallen in love instead. So there I was at the start of a new school year with a new love and no teaching position. By November the need to be in a classroom pushed me, a little reluctantly, a lot excitedly, through the doors of the local School for Retarded Children.

"Good morning. I'd like to do some volunteer work. I'm a teacher. I've only taught high school English. But maybe you have something. . . ."

Life skills. What the hell are they? Just what skills would I pass on in the name of success? happiness? independence?

I was given a lesson in behavior modification and told that although cleanliness may no longer hold its place next to godliness, it would sure be nice if the girls acquired some basic skills in good grooming.

Source: Reprinted from *Educational Leadership* (November 1981). Copyright © 1981 by the Association for Supervision and Curriculum Development, Alexandria, Virginia.

Teaching & Joy

That first morning, in preparation for classes, I carefully braided my hair, weaving a bright scarlet ribbon into the strands. My nails matched my lipstick. I chose to wear a white dress splashed with small pink roses. It was a simple dress of easy-to-sew cotton. I hoped it was soft and feminine and appealing. During the lunch hour, I proceeded to cut out an apron of matching material. The next day, I sewed a hem. Finally, on went a piece of lace, and the dress was ready to wear during "break time" when we toasted tea cakes and made rich chocolate milks and sipped them in the finest china I could find. In fact, it was an antique set my great grandmother had brought from Germany. We used linen napkins and silver spoons. Each day I brought fresh flowers for our table. I didn't talk much about washing hair or feeling good about oneself. I didn't show films on it or give sewing lessons. But suddenly the girls were braiding one another's hair. And when it didn't shine, they were washing and rinsing and conditioning. Heirloom dishes are always carefully washed. Linen napkins deserve ironing and folding. Silver spoons and tea pots warrant a shine, a polish, a making of funny faces into.

Pieces of ribbon and lace and soft cotton appeared, and sewing machines started whirring. It was amongst those sporadically running, racing, stopping, starting again machines that I came to know Eileen, came to recognize the large soft body moving noisily between the girls, the rich, soothing voice encouraging, laughing, admiring.

As is the case with so many handicapped children, Eileen suffered from many ailments, including diabetes and arthritis. Despite the fact that swelling and pain demanded daily visits from the nurse, who applied ice and weights to Eileen's legs, and despite the fact her fingers curled in painful distortions, Eileen was never deterred from helping a shaky friend thread a needle, or organizing the younger children into a game on the playground. I saw Eileen suffer more than any child I'd ever known, but I never heard her complain, never once, and often I heard her laugh. But even more, I heard her assure, encourage, assist, and sometimes insist. I saw her believe in herself and in those around her.

One afternoon, in desperation and fatigue, the nurse complained to Eileen, "But, Eileen, why ever didn't you tell us about the pain in your legs before it got so bad? We could have helped you so much more if you had. Next time, for heaven's sake, tell somebody."

Eileen's eyes filled with tears. The nurse returned to her V.O.N. van. Eileen and I talked. "She didn't mean to make you sad, Eileen. She just hates to see you hurt so much. It's easier to help someone when they first get sick. Telling a nurse or someone who can help is a good thing to do. No one gets angry when you're sick. Everyone just wants to help." My meaningless words ran on.

Eileen listened patiently. When I was finished, she looked at me quietly. Her voice shook a little as she spoke. "But I was at home."

"Home?" My voice was full of surprise. "But surely you could have told your mother?"

"No." Quietly.

"No?" Still not understanding.

"No." A pause. "She was too sad already."

I rubbed Eileen's legs for an extra long time that day. It felt good to touch her. We didn't say much. We just looked at each other and smiled a lot.

I guess we became a team. It was my first team-teaching experience. It was my best.

Together, with Eileen modeling, encouraging, expecting, understanding much more than I, we moved through what became a rather mobile life skills program. Reading lessons from basal texts were never given. But recipes and instructions on sewing patterns were carefully followed. Safety rules never appeared in bright posters on the walls. We had no time to make posters. We were busy catching buses, walking to stores, shopping for chocolate and croissants, and matching ribbons and laces. Math was never really part of any formal lesson, but when we sold homemade popcorn balls and handsewn aprons to earn extra shopping money, we sure checked out prices and counted change. I saw Eileen help an 8-year-old count her money four times before she was content to leave a frowning clerk, who somehow felt compelled to endure the painstaking procedure. His annoyance didn't rattle Eileen a bit; it was

Jody's uncertainty at having the right change that concerned her. And with that she carefully, patiently dealt.

That day, as I watched Eileen direct Jody in the counting of change, it occurred to me that what I was witnessing, indeed, what we were doing, was organic teaching. I hurried home, reread *Teacher*, and recharged my teaching batteries.

Classical music became a part of our tea-time pleasure. It wasn't long before we were able to delight one another, and quite frankly, ourselves, with our own music. I played the instrument of my childhood, the piano. The rest of the girls improvised in glorious harmony and mood on Orff instruments.

And with music, naturally, came dance. We danced, we read the life story of Isadora, and we saw the movie with Vanessa Redgrave. I guess we all became more beautiful that year.

Finally, sadly and with happiness, the year ended, and my not-so-new love and I did move to Florida in order for me to continue with that promised learning. Each Christmas I sent Eileen a small present. Each Christmas I missed her more. Eileen, the snow, the smell of pine, bits of ribbon, Eileen. Each Christmas.

In 1979, the present was returned to me. With it came a note from Eileen's mother. "I'm sorry. Thank you for sending this, but Eileen passed away this winter."

I wrote back. I think I talked about sorrow and loss. Somewhere I mentioned gratitude. Did I know enough to really tell her of her gift to the world, and to me? Somehow did that woman come to understand the inspiration, the magic that was and is her daughter?

> Children have two visions, the inner and the outer.
> Of the two the inner vision is brighter.
>
> —Sylvia Ashton-Warner
> *Teacher*

Carolyn Mamchur was a mother, wife, high school teacher, and university student by her 20th birthday. She left Canada for Florida to earn a doctorate in education in 1976 and begin her writing career working with the Southern author Harry Crews. She is now an Associate Professor at Simon Fraser University, Burnaby, B.C., Canada, and President of her own company. Mamchur gives extensive lectures and workshops on writing process, Jungian type theory, implementation processes, motivational needs and stress management, and organizational development. She is the author of several books and screenplays.

Sheila Feigelson shares remedies for the Humor Deprivation Syndrome that exists in some of our organizations.

11

Increase Your Laugh Life!

BY SHEILA FEIGELSON

"Sometimes I think I'm indecisive, but I'm not so sure!"

"Smile! Give your face a break!"

"The next best thing to solving a problem is finding some humor in it."

These signs of our times send us urgent messages to loosen up, lighten up, and not take ourselves so seriously. Adding a little humor to our daily diet can help us feel better as we take the weight of the world off our shoulders.

Any diet is harder to follow when we're feeling hassled by pressures at work and home, but that's just when we need to pay attention most—when we are irritated, annoyed, or frustrated.

Humor may be our most powerful natural resource for dealing with life's little upsets. Our sense of humor and ability to laugh with others, at ourselves, and at situations is what keeps us in balance.

The positive effect of a "humor diet" has been well documented by numerous writers and speakers. Author Norman Cousins described in his best-selling book, *Anatomy of an Illness,* how a good amount of laughter helped him

recover from a painful life-threatening illness. Along with appropriate medical care and the support of family and friends, Cousins proclaims that humor and laughter played a significant role in his recovery. When he laughed hard for 10 minutes, he was able to enjoy two hours of pain-free sleep.

We feel better when we laugh and smile. Humor is good for our health. It's a powerful tool for communicating many kinds of messages, coping with tension and stress, and building relationships. In fact, pianist-comedian Victor Borge reminds us that "A smile is the shortest distance between two people!"

Inviting Laughter and Smiles

Just as we go on a planned diet to eat healthy foods, so can we design a diet to invite healthy laughter. Expanding our sense of humor can enhance the pleasure of being together and reduce the effects of stress.

Each of us can do things to keep our sense of humor alive and well. Joel Goodman, founder and director of the internationally acclaimed Humor Project in Saratoga Springs, New York, points out that humor is "a set of skills, attitudes, and guidelines that we can consciously access, and like any set of skills, humor can be nurtured through practice." To help us do that, the Humor Project sponsors an annual conference on the "Positive Power of Humor and Creativity," which attracts more than 1,000 people from all over the United States and other parts of the world.

You don't necessarily have to attend a conference, however, to develop and practice your humor skills. You can incorporate humor and invite laughter into your own life and into the lives of others by doing some simple, free, or inexpensive things. Some examples are (1) talk about fun topics; (2) keep funny stuff around you; (3) and be on the lookout for opportunities.

Conversation Topics

By topics, we don't mean jokes. You do not have to become a stand-up comedian to invite laughter. Instead, you can steer the conversation to a subject you know will evoke a smile and keep things on a positive track.

65

Conversations about pleasant childhood experiences and recollections are bound to cause smiles, regardless of age. Talking about how we entertained ourselves when we were young makes us remember good times, and when we share these out loud with others, the chances increase for a hearty laugh.

In meeting or classroom settings, one of the easiest ways to charge an atmosphere with "positivity" is to have people create name tags on which they indicate a favorite childhood game or toy in addition to their own name. As people respond, they smile; you can hardly recall a fun memory without chuckling. Remembering favorite comedians has a similar effect. Typically, when we talk about a favorite funny person, we talk about something they do that makes us laugh, and we laugh all over again. Describing a humorous cartoon does the same thing.

Other topics to tickle the funny bone and build relationships include clothing fads from high school, popular songs from our school days, favorite childhood candies, "weird" food combinations, embarrassing moments, "dumb" things we used to do, silly fears we had, and funny signs we've seen. These can be woven into our conversations at appropriate times.

Funny Stuff and Props

Displaying humorous objects is an easy way to increase your laugh life and reduce tension. One principal describes how he keeps a couple of small wind-up toys and other trinkets on his desk. Such items help make people comfortable and add some lightness to an otherwise serious conversation. Often, while business is being discussed, visitors pick one up and play with it as they talk. At home, you could add some toys or gimmicks to your coffee table to encourage amusement for yourself and your guests.

A busy secretary's work space displays this message: "You may know where you're going, God may know where you're going, but does your secretary know where you're going?" What a gentle way to say, "Where are you going and when will you be back?" With a bit of modification, parents could use this message with their teenagers as well.

Classified ads can be a source of humor. When clipped and copied for others, they can invite shared laughter. Two favorites are "LOST: Wristwatch, second-hand missing, winder loose, glass cracked. $3.00 reward if returned in perfect condition" and "FOR SALE: Business site at busy intersection, with traffic light frequently out of order. Perfect spot for doctor or lawyer!"

All kinds of buttons and T-shirt logos can be worn just for the purpose of encouraging others to smile with you. One of my favorites is, "Wear A Smile, One Size Fits All."

To help family members stay on the sunny side, one mother keeps a bottle of "Grouch Control Pills™" on the window ledge over the kitchen sink. The label on the pills, which are really jellybeans, reads, "Take one after each growl, frown, complaint, or scowl to control grouchiness. Warning: Serious side effects of an occasional smile or grin may occur."

Displaying humorous objects at work or at home sends a message that basically says, "I'm approachable. I enjoy myself. Join me in laughter and smiles." And keeping humorous items in your purse or wallet or on your desk is a wonderful way to amuse yourself and be prepared for that moment when a bit of levity is needed.

Try doing a "Humor Inventory" some time. Look through your purse, wallet, pockets, briefcase, and desk drawers. What do you have that makes you smile? Chances are you will chuckle as you go on this "Humor Hunt," and when you tell someone else about what you found, you will double the enjoyment. A good way to open is merely to say, "Guess what I found in my desk drawer today."

Watch for Opportunities

If you look for opportunities for humor, they will find you. Our daily routines provide many situations for lightness and laughter. For instance, when you travel, be aware of the humorous bumper stickers, billboards, and advertisements on the sides of vehicles. A sanitation truck was spotted with a sign that read: "Satisfaction Guaranteed or Double Your Rubbish Back!" A plumber's truck reads: "A Flush Beats A Full House." And on a billboard advertising an engineering company: "Precision Engineering Company—103 Yards, 2 Feet, 9 Inches Away."

When shopping, be aware of funny signs like this one that appeared in a novelty jewelry store: "Ears Pierced . . . While You Wait." And the sign in a restaurant announcing, "Special Today: T-Bone, $0.70. With meat, $18.50."

Humor can help us soften negative messages like "No parking," "No eating inside," or "No smoking." The universal "no" sign, with a circle and a slash, has become widely recognized. One clever 12-year-old used this international non-verbal language on a poster for his father, who habitually falls asleep in front of the TV and snores loudly. The sign reads: "No snoring zone! $500 fine. ZZzzzz." To soften the "No parking" message, one company posted this sign: "If there is not a big heavy green tow truck here now, there will be shortly!" Humor can give negative messages more impact and make them easier to accept.

Tardiness is often a problem in schools, meetings, and social settings. One employee, who was habitually late, arrived at work in a rabbit outfit, yelling, "I'm late, I'm late." Everyone laughed. The boss saved his lecture on punctuality, and the employee saved his job—this time. Collecting overdue bills is a real pain for many organizations. Some people let go of frustration just by *thinking* of including the following note with statements to past-due clients: "Please let us be your pallbearer when you die. We've carried you this long, and we'd like the privilege of doing so to the end."

When visiting people who are sick, you have opportunities for bringing smiles at an especially important time. Although flowers and cards are always nice to send, consider giving something humorous. One woman prepares a container of candy kisses and includes a note that reads, "These will have to do until I can give you the real thing!" Another person reported that her hospital stay and subsequent convalescence was much more manageable with the help of friends who called each day with humorous stories.

Sometimes we would just like to be left alone for a while, both at work and at home. "Don't disturb me . . . I'm disturbed enough already" reads this

light-hearted sign on one manager's door. His teenage daughter posted it on her bedroom door at home to gently give the same message to the family.

During the day, we all have times when we wait. Humor can help us deal with long or short waiting periods, whether at a meeting, in the doctor's office, in traffic jams, or at the grocery store. Having something humorous to listen to in the car, to read while sitting, or to actually put on (such as a funny mask or Groucho Glasses) can help reduce tension caused by waiting. With a bit of planning, we can actually turn those negative, stress-producing moments into more positive ones. In his book, *The Healing Power of Humor,* humor specialist and author Allen Klein reminds us that a bit of preplanned humor is like having a psychological insurance policy: "You may never need it, but it sure is nice to know it's there if you do."

To increase your laugh life, expand your humor awareness level. Your effort will be well rewarded . . . soon!

Sheila Feigelson speaks and writes about putting humor to work in meetings, organizations, and everyday life. Feigelson is a former junior high school teacher and instructor of student teachers at the University of Michigan, and lives in Ann Arbor.

Teaching with joy is not for the faint of heart. In this beautiful story, the late Judy-Arin Krupp reminds us of the importance of commitment and perseverance to any task we choose to undertake. Her own life was a wonderful example of how to live with commitment, determination, humor, and joy.

12

Learning That Came Alive on Heartbreak Hill

BY JUDY-ARIN KRUPP

The sign, written in black marker on white sheeting, hung over a nursing home. My legs felt heavy. My pace had slowed. Under the banner sat senior citizens in wheelchairs. The printed words burned into my psyche, giving me renewed strength. My stride quickened. At age 52, nearing the end of this, my first marathon, a marathon for which I was not assiduously prepared, I hurt everywhere—even places I didn't know I had. My senses had dulled, so I neither saw nor heard the cheering crowd. Yet, the words on that sign continued to drive my legs: *Life's A Marathon, Be In It.*

Little did I realize, as I crossed the finish line, that a deeper message would evolve for me over the years. Now, four years, six marathons, three hikes to the summit of mountains between 14,334 and 20,000 feet, and many long-distance bike trips later, those words have a profound meaning for me.

Each actual marathon I've run, all 26.2 miles, as well as other endurance events, requires sensible and committed training—long and short runs, speed work, appropriate food and rest; putting one foot in front of the other and taking it step by step; pacing; and a mind-set that says, "I can."

Is this different from the requirements of sitting a daily vigil at the bedside of a seriously ill loved one? I recently did just that. My 87-year-old mother had aortic valve replacement and bypass surgery. I stayed at Mom's side for days without knowing if she would survive. I continued to exercise, eat sensibly, rest, and seek support. I dealt with one trauma at a time as each developed. I maintained my perspective by taking breaks to work, cook, or read, which helped me keep going when I felt overwhelmed by the possibility of Mom's death. Last, I had a positive mind-set. I believed Mom had the strength and will to survive, but if she did not live, then I knew I had the resilience to keep her memory alive by living fully.

Mom both survived and thrived. At the age of 88, this feisty lady continues to run circles around many of us. She baked two pies and made a company dinner just $2\frac{1}{2}$ months post surgery, she goes from store to store to get the best prices on groceries, she drives, and she volunteers at the local hospital. And, she now deals with her own marathon, coping with a husband who has had a number of strokes and has lost mental capacity. He exhibits irrational anger and paranoia, which he often directs at her. He imagines things, gets lost, bad-mouths family members, threatens to leave, and forgets the water running in the kitchen. Mom contends she handles the difficulties better when she has eaten well, exercised, and rested. She says, "I'll just take it one day at a time." She paces herself, making sure she has rested in the afternoon because Dad's worse in the early evening. Mom believes she can handle Dad because, "I love him and I feel so badly for him."

Life is a marathon and, want to or not, we participate in it by dint of living. Life's marathons include having a very bad class for a year and maintaining your patience and love of children; giving birth to and raising a child with a chronic physical or psychological problem; discovering one of your children has chosen a lifestyle the antithesis of yours; driving a car that continually breaks down when you cannot afford a new vehicle; surviving a messy divorce that your partner initiated; working in a job that no longer feels challenging but having so much invested in a retirement plan that you feel you can't leave; and _____ (please add a marathon of your own to the list). Each marathon requires preparation, taking one step at a time, pacing, and a positive mind-set. At the same time, each marathon teaches something new. What have the marathons of my life taught me?

Climbing to 17,000 feet on Mount Kilimanjaro, I blacked out momentarily. At 18,760 feet, with only 50 percent of the oxygen available at sea level, I developed double vision and dizziness. Yet, I made it to the summit. My desire to reach Gilman's Point was so great that I persevered and learned that every endurance event brings negative feelings, and real physical pain or difficulty. When the goal pulls with magnetic force, then it seems natural and comfortable to push to reach that goal.

How many teachers persist with a tough class because their goal of helping the students learn and adjust acts like a magnet? Does Mom continue to work with Dad because she feels the pull of her value system? Do the parents of a child with ADD (attention deficit disorder) struggle to help their child because they envision the child leading a quality life?

I responsibly trained for the second marathon and had a quality run. I cut 27 minutes off the time for my first marathon and had a "kick" left at the end for the video camera held by one of my children. My family cheered and had orange juice ready for me at two critical points along the course. One of my daughters ran the last six miles with me. Two insights emerged. First, appropriate readiness makes the marathon easier. Second, seeking support eases the strain and pain of stressful life experiences. How often in my life had I "stood on my own two feet" and "gutted it out," rather than appear weak by asking for aid? How foolish of me not to say, "I need help," especially from those with whom I share love.

Preparedness for a marathon comes from pounding the pavement during daily runs. Readiness for life's marathons comes through studying, learning

from others, observing, planning, communicating effectively, making decisions, and maintaining a sense of humor.

Seeking support during a marathon does not differ from seeking support during the marathon of life. Adults need to ask for help. How many people with cancer join support groups and find that marathon easier? How many senior citizens move at an even, steady pace, secure in the support of family and friends they can call on for a ride to the store, a family dinner, or any other reason that comes along? People who seek support demonstrate their self-respect. They honor themselves by recognizing their need and acting on it. I needed my children's backing and asked them to join me on the running course.

During the descent from the glaciated summit of Mount Rainier's 14,344 feet, the snow had softened and our crampons (metal spikes that fit on hiking hooks) caked with slush and became slippery. We came to one of the many crevasses I'd jumped easily on our ascent. Now I felt fear. The slippery snow prompted me to say to myself, "You'd best use care or you'll fall." Sure enough, I fell three feet into the crevasse. With help, I extricated myself and stood on firm ice with spaghetti legs and a pounding heart. I had to overcome the feeling of, "I can't do this" in order to successfully traverse the remaining 13,000 feet. I talked to myself saying, "Judy, you are capable. You can flawlessly make it down and have fun doing so." I imagined myself successfully leaping over other crevasses. As a result, I had no further problems, got silly, and had fun during the descent. I learned more about the psychic features of the marathon of life. I had often mouthed the words, "What you think is what you get." Now, I believed them. I thought I might fall, and I did. I began to understand how easily I talk myself into or out of situations and feelings. The power of positive thinking became clear.

Life's marathon requires a mind-set that says, "I can." Backing from loved ones, friends, and acquaintances helps reach that mind-set. Teachers who believe they can reach children will use different approaches, constantly try to improve methodologies, and will perceive defeats as opportunities for growth. Those with an "I can" philosophy will look at a knotty problem at work from diverse perspectives in hopes of discovering a solution. When an approach doesn't work, they will try a different tact, thus increasing their chance for success.

The 1992 New York and Boston marathons provided me with role models, with people to emulate, people from whom to learn. Fred Lebow, the man who organized and ran the New York Marathon, worked for years to recover enough from a malignant brain tumor to run again. Gretta Weitz, a world-class runner, chose to run with Fred. Her love and his determination resulted in mobs of people cheering them on and the joy of Fred Lebow finishing the race.

Similarly, in 1992, Johnny Kelley completed his 61st Boston Marathon at the age of 84. As I passed him during the run, I thanked him for his participation and told him how much he inspired me. When I began to feel the misery of having burned my glycogen stores and needing to burn fat, I thought of Johnny Kelley. "If he can do it at 84, what is my problem at 55?" A sculpture erected in his honor on Heartbreak Hill (at the 19–20 mile mark in the race, running becomes more difficult; so "hearts break" when runners see the hill ahead) shows two figures running hand in hand to the finish line. One figure represents Johnny Kelley when he won Boston in 1935, and the other figure shows Johnny Kelley when he completed his last race. This unique "metaphor for the spirit of our youth running with us throughout life" provides a role model for all people.

These three people taught me great lessons. Gretta Weitz taught the meaning of love. She did not compete in the 1992 New York Marathon. Instead, she ran at Fred Lebow's slow speed. She offered him her love and support. After the race, she said it was the hardest race she had ever run because it required her to go at a painfully slow pace. How many times have we felt discomfort doing something for, or with, another in their style? Yet how vital in the marathon of life to continue to do this for one another.

Fred Lebow taught me about determination. I know what it feels like to run a marathon when in good health. I can only imagine the pain, anguish, tenacity, and euphoria that accompany a runner in ill health. When I feel like quitting, I think of Fred and find renewed strength.

Johnny Kelley reinforced my belief in keeping the child within alive. He ran as a youth. He ran as a senior citizen. He allowed the spirit of his youth to stay with him throughout his life. He helps me believe in my ability to keep active psychologically and physically as I age.

Mother's six-month bout with heart disease and her ultimate surgery provided me with much time to think. I realized she will never die, but will always live on in my heart. I became aware of just how many of her values and beliefs I had integrated into my sense of self. Her illness gave me an opportunity to do anticipatory grieving. To ready myself for her death, I cried, I laughed, I shared stories about Mom with others, and I relived much of my youth. Most of all, I realized I will survive her death despite a great sense of loss.

How many people living with the marathon of their own imminent death need to cry, laugh, share stories, and accept the inevitable? How many people losing anything (spouse, child to marriage, job, youth, or great 2nd grade class) need to do the same?

Each life marathon and each actual marathon provide opportunities for learning. I never dreamed a simple piece of sheeting hanging from a nursing home would affect my life so profoundly. This lesson, as with so many in life, came when I least expected it. The meaning inherent in the sign became more clear to me with each marathon of life I experienced. I suspect more significant insights about the message, *Life's A Marathon, Be In It,* await me.

Judy-Arin Krupp was killed in 1994 by a tractor trailer as she stood next to her bicycle on the side of a highway. Before her untimely death, she was an international expert in adult development, adult learning, self-esteem, change, staff development, and stress.

Krupp wrote three books: Adult Development: Implications for Staff Development, The Adult Learner: A Unique Entity, *and* When Parents Face the Schools. *She also wrote numerous articles for professional journals and books, covering such topics as motivating experienced employees, self-esteem, mentoring, a holistic view of adult learners, and learning styles.*

Krupp was an ardent bicyclist, marathon runner, and mountain climber. She taught every grade from nursery school through graduate school, and established and ran her own business.

"Oh good, we're having another adventure!" Sometimes children are the teachers.

13

Child's Play: Making Molehills Out of Mountains

BY ALLEN KLEIN

Children have a remarkable talent for not treating the adult world with the kind of respect we are so confident it ought to be given. To the irritation of authority figures of all sorts, children expend considerable energy in "clowning around." They refuse to appreciate the gravity of our monumental concerns, while we forget that if we were to become more like children, our concerns might not be so monumental.

—*Conrad Hyers*

"One evening," writes Richard Lewis in the magazine *Parabola*, "I went out to have dinner at a Japanese restaurant. I sat near two children, about 6 or 7 years old. Amidst the refinement of a beautifully set table, the voices of these children were about to alter the mood of the setting:

Source: Adapted by permission of The Putnam Publishing Group/Jeremy P. Tarcher, Inc., from *The Healing Power of Humor* by Allen Klein. Copyright © 1989 by Allen Klein.

"First Child: 'Why did the girl blush when she opened the refrigerator door?'

"Second Child: 'Because she saw the salad dressing.'

"Grins, a burst of giggles, and a warm laugh from everyone within hearing—and the world, for the moment, had somehow righted itself again."

Children are an important source for righting ourselves when we feel like crying. They have a unique way of looking at the world. Their perspective can teach adults an important lesson: Burdens can become less weighty when we use our imaginations to play with our problems.

Our imaginations are wonderful tools for turning our troubles around. We can use our childlike imagination to play with any unpleasant occurrence or turn any task into a game.

To a child, everything is a game. The world is a huge playground. Play is a vital element in a child's development. When we are growing up, we learn about the subtleties and complexities of our surroundings through play. As adults, we forget that play, be it mental or physical, can once more help us deal with our world. It can change our energy, provide relief from our problems, and even help us find solutions to them.

Making a game out of a difficult task or situation turns it into play. The world, and everything in it, therefore, becomes an adult playground, too.

Dr. O. Carl Simonton, coauthor of *Getting Well Again,* says that "play is essential for life. . . . It is not selective, it is mandatory." Simonton is so convinced of the value of play that he teaches juggling to cancer patients. He says that play takes our mind away from our problems. If you think about your illness—or any other difficulty, for that matter—while juggling, you will drop the ball.

In my workshops, I get people moving around the room doing things like jumping up and down, shouting out the last digit of their phone number, and making the letter "H" with their bodies. Much laughter and a sense of renewed vitality occur in the room after these exercises. The games illustrate how quickly play changes our energy. By playing around with those things that annoy us and turning them into a game, we change the energy we have toward our upsets, we free our creativity, and we help solve our problems.

Cheryl Thorn, a mother of three, said that she frequently saw her children use games to turn their upsets around. When her oldest daughter was 4, Cheryl noticed that whenever one particular friend came over to play, no one fought. So one day she asked her daughter, "Iyan, how come when Adam comes over you two never fight?"

Iyan replied, "Adam showed me a game to play whenever we start to argue. We put our hands together and push against each other. It makes us laugh, so we never fight."

Cheryl's two other children have also shown her how to counteract upsets and fears with play. When Mariana, her youngest, was learning to ride a bicycle, she frequently fell. One day, Cheryl noticed Julian come over, put his arms around Mariana, and shake her. Then both of them vigorously stamped their feet on the ground. Julian informed Cheryl that they were shaking and stamping out Mariana's scared feelings.

Dr. Simonton emphasizes the need for physical play. I believe that mental play is mandatory, too. Instead of logically trying to figure out the solution to a problem—and often getting stuck when no solution seems feasible—allowing ourselves to play in our imagination can often lead to a solution. Adults forget that the creative child's mind is still within us and that, like children, we can use our imaginations to change our perceptions of the things that annoy and trouble us.

Children use their imaginations to become whomever they want to be and to transport themselves to wherever they want to go. You can do the same thing to help pick yourself up when you are down. By playing in your mind, you can eliminate what you do not like and re-create what you want.

Imagine yourself in a job in which you deal with the public throughout the day. Suddenly an irate person comes over and starts yelling at you. One way to keep your perspective and not get involved in the ranting and raving is to use your imagination and mentally play with the situation. A receptionist in a probation office relates that when incidents like this occur to her—and they often do—she uses some mental play. She thinks of people as animal types. "They might come to me as grizzly bears, but I soften them by seeing them as teddy bears."

Sometimes mind play can lead to actual humorous solutions to our problems and help make molehills out of mountains. One homemaker, for example, used her imagination to counteract her husband's constant complaints about getting the same thing for lunch every day. He opened his lunch box one day to discover that his wife had filled it with a coconut and a hammer.

Some people have used their playful imaginations to turn annoyances into games. One woman said she makes a game of her work by setting quotas for herself and then trying to surpass them. She gives herself a gold star for each sale she makes; for every 10 sales, she sends herself a bouquet of flowers.

Seminar leader Jim Pelley turns parking his car into a game. He says that when he gets frustrated trying to find a space, "I imagine that there is one and only one available, and it is my goal to find it."

William Daniels, a college professor from Schenectady, New York, made a game out of getting his students to show up for their finals. Over a period of years, he had his exams either delivered by helicopter, embedded in a chunk of ice, or baked in cookies.

A childlike view of the world can frequently put adult life in perspective. In a small book titled *Don't Cross Your Bridge Before. . .*, 1st grade teacher Judith Frost Stark gives us a glimpse of the way children often think:

> A penny saved . . . is not much.
> Opportunity only knocks when . . . she can't reach the doorbell.
> When the cat's away . . . no pooh!

In *The Joy of Working,* authors Denis Waitley and Reni Witt suggest that we go through our day as if doing everything for the first time, like a child might. "When faced with a routine—typing letters, answering the telephone, selling door-to-door, filling out forms—approach each task as if it were your first time."

Ann, a woman in one of my workshops, told me how her young son helped her get a new perspective on her upsets. She was having one setback after another: She recently separated from her husband; her place of business closed; her car conked out. Just when she thought she could not handle one more thing, her water heater exploded—no significant damage, but a horrible mess. As she was about to begin the major cleanup, her young son burst into the room, saw what happened, and exclaimed, "Oh, good, we're having another adventure!"

Even as adults, we can tap into our inner child's sense of adventure and unique way of seeing the world. We were all children once, and some part of us still is. Some part within is still wanting to say the things we are not supposed to say, wanting to run through the halls of the library or take off our shoes and play in the sandbox. And while many of the things children get away with are inappropriate for adults, children can still teach us much about freeing ourselves from our burdens.

Whether we use our imaginations to alter our upsets or add some play element to our painful situations, 10 seconds of child's play is sometimes all it takes to shift our focus from the dark moments to the lighter ones.

Allen Klein offers award-winning presentations on the power of humor in our daily lives. He is the author of The Healing Power of Humor, *published by Jeremy P. Tarcher, Putnam,* Quotations to Cheer You Up, *and* Wing Tips. *He refers to himself as the "Jolly-tologist," and his writings and public presentations certainly lend credence to his claim.*

Klein is a Certified Speaking Professional member of the National Speakers Association and currently resides in San Francisco (telephone: 415-431-1913).

The relationship between a teacher and a student offers special gifts to each. Caryn Edwards describes her special gift.

14

The Birthday Card

BY CARYN EDWARDS

When I first began tutoring Clark in reading, I was impressed by his keen desire to learn to read. Clark was 56 years old and could only recognize the letters in his first name and print them in unorthodox fashion. All his life he had wanted to learn to read; but none of the programs had worked for him, including public school education, adult basic education, and numerous literacy programs.

During our initial session, I asked him what his goal was in reading—what did he want to achieve by learning to read? Clark told me that he wanted to be able to read the Bible. Knowing what a difficult reading task the Bible can be even for high-level readers, I realized my work was cut out for me. On the positive side, I had a highly motivated student, unwilling to give up even after numerous failures in other literacy programs.

Clark proved to be one of the most dedicated students I had ever worked with. He did daily homework before he went to his regular job. Monday through Friday, he would set his alarm for 5 a.m. to allow an hour of study before heading out to his construction job. He also worked on weekends. Clark had a severe learning disability, and even though the multisensory approach was

working, he needed many reinforcing activities and lots of practice—his progress was painfully slow. But he never complained and was always enthusiastic and diligent during our sessions.

The first real breakthrough came several months after we had begun our work together. One night Clark arrived early, which wasn't unusual, but he seemed agitated. I could tell that he had something important to tell me; however, he didn't seem comfortable volunteering the information. Therefore, I progressed through the lesson as usual, waiting patiently for his news. Clark was so anxious that I was afraid he would quit. Finally, at the end of our session, Clark asked if we could talk. I said, "Sure, what's on your mind, Clark?"

"Something very important happened to me yesterday, Caryn, and I need to tell you about it," he said. "It was my wife's birthday, so I went to the card shop for the first time to buy her a card," Clark began. "We have been married for over 30 years, and for the very first time in my life I was actually able to find a birthday card for her. First, I went to the section that started with "B's" and I sounded out *birthday*. I have never been able to do that before, but yesterday I did it because you taught me about *b, ir, th, d, ay*."

While Clark was telling me this, his eyes were aimed straight down at his shoes, but now he paused and looked right into my eyes and said, "Thank you." Tears were in his eyes and I felt my own glistening. I cannot recall a happier, more rewarding moment in my teaching career. I had given Clark the gift of the written word, and he had used that gift to bestow a gift of love on his wife by selecting her birthday card.

Clark and I seemed to reach a new level of friendship after that day. He began bringing me a small token of thanks at each lesson. One time it would be donuts, once raspberries, sometimes cookies, or tomatoes, or flowers from his garden. We shared many happy moments as he discovered the world through the written word, and I rejoiced in each new skill he mastered.

I wonder if Clark ever knew that he had already given me the greatest gift a student can give a teacher when he allowed me to share in his joy and self-pride as he learned to read. The last time I saw Clark we read from the Bible together, but the memory of his learning struggles and his accomplishments

remains and often provides a special strength that I can call upon when facing the many challenges of teaching a new "slow learner" to read.

Caryn Edwards has been involved in education for more than 30 years. She has been a special education teacher and regular education teacher, a tutor for private organizations, an administrator, and a trainer of educators. She has also been an active volunteer in the field. Edwards is the Immediate Past President of the Learning Disabilities Association of Michigan; Vice President of the Capitol Area ADD Network; and a past board member on the Michigan Branch of the Orton Dyslexia Society, Mid-Michigan Easter Seal Society, and Lekotek. She currently is Vice Chairman of the Special Education Advisory Committee to the State Board of Education and is a board member of the National Board for the Learning Disabilities Association of America. She is Director of the Erickson Learning Center and the Erickson Learning Foundation in Okemos, Michigan.

Edwards has presented at many state conferences, including CEC, LDA of Michigan, Michigan School Testing Conference, Michigan Alternative Education Conference, CHADD State Conference, and Compensatory Education State Conference. She has also presented at the International Learning Disabilities Association of America. In addition, she has trained thousands of teachers throughout Michigan through in-service programs and workshops in public and private education.

Edwards is married and has two children. Reading is her favorite pastime. Therefore, teaching others to read is the job she enjoys most.

15

Find Your Joy by Following Your Heart

BY DEBORAH ROZMAN

"Heart" is a word that describes many things. On a physical level, the heart pumps blood through the body. We look to the heart as a source of wisdom when we say, "Go deep in your heart for an answer," and a source of power when we say, "Put your heart into it." The heart is sung about, talked about, philosophized about, and is at the core of every religion. But what is the heart, really? Webster's dictionary defines the heart as the center of the total personality, especially with reference to intuition, feeling, or emotion, and as a source of strength and courage. At the Institute of HeartMath (IHM), we have spent more than a decade studying the nature of the heart to understand what facilitates people's happiness and fulfillment. Our psychological and scientific research has uncovered the heart as a source of both intelligence and power. Subtle heart feelings are what unlock the doorway to insight, self-empowerment, and the joy of discovery.

Our research with children and adults over the last 15 years has shown us that true, lasting learning involves a balance of both heart and head. Society, however, has increasingly placed an overemphasis on head knowledge at the expense of the heart. As a result, learning in school has dropped. Fewer children are motivated to learn; and for many, school is boring, dry, and joyless.

Despite high-tech achievements, we have a society of children at risk. Our educational programs do not adequately prepare children for today's turbulent and stressful world. And estimates now show that one in four adolescents is extremely vulnerable to substance abuse, sexual promiscuity, and criminal violence. A recent National Assessment of Educational Progress (NAEP) also concluded that "students at all grade levels are deficient in higher-order thinking skills." Millions are leaving school with no job training and little hope. Children's needs in our rapidly changing society are not being met. Few schools pay attention to the emotional or social development of students, then wonder why they are alienated and uninterested in learning basic skills. How can the heart help break through this social and educational quagmire?

Lack of heart connection has caused many youngsters and adults to end up misplaced and unhappy. We are a society of "looking good and feeling bad." Though our inner worlds may be emotionally unbalanced and unfulfilled, and our thinking processes often uncontrolled, self-negating, or angry, we make sure we look good—and sound good—even though we may be isolated and hurting. When mental and emotional processes are not managed and out of balance, the heart—our source of connection and communion with others—shuts down.

There are simple solutions, but they require changing the underlying premises and paradigms in which we operate. They involve building a deeper and more meaningful connection to our own hearts and to other people. The compassion, clarity, energy, and problem-solving skills required to create fundamental systemic changes reside in the positive feelings associated with the human heart.

Joy, love, care, and appreciation are powerful motivators. They are all *feelings* that humans experience around the heart. Joy is a feeling of pleasure or delight that arises from the heart. Positive feelings are what make life worth living. At the Institute of HeartMath, we have discovered an equation for accelerated learning: Feeling + Perception = Understanding. What this means is that your *understanding* of any subject, problem, or issue is determined by your perception of it, and perception is colored by feeling. If your feeling is one of anger, boredom, frustration, or distress, perception of the issue is distorted and so is understanding. If your feeling is one of peace, joy, love, or appreciation for the subject, perception clears and understanding unfolds. Furthermore, when you understand a subject at both the feeling and head levels, you experience the joy of insight—the joy of discovery and learning.

HeartMath research has shown that positive feelings in the heart are a person's source of intuitive knowing. When we feel joy, peace, care, or appreciation, we access a wider perspective of intuitive understanding. The mind expands, leading us to creative ideas and commonsense solutions to problems. Our own intelligence would tell us that when we feel frustrated, angry, self-judging, or miserable, the heart shuts down, stress hormones are released throughout the body, our perspective narrows, and it's hard to focus on anything. Furthermore, scientific studies have proven that negative emotions suppress the immune system and can lead to hypertension or stress-related illnesses; positive emotions increase the efficiency of the heart, bolster the immune response, and release stress on contact.

Understanding the psychological and scientific function of joy and other positive emotions in the learning process is critical for educators in the '90s. With increasing social pressures on teachers, parents, and children, negative emotions are on the rampage, blocking children's learning ability, as well as our competence as adults to parent or teach effectively. The ability to mentally and emotionally manage one's inner life has never been widely recognized as the most basic of human skills. Yet this area is where each one of us experiences the joy or pain of our own life. HeartMath brings this inner mental and emotional balancing process to the table.

Who would have thought that a major answer to our educational dilemma is mental and emotional balance, along with the rekindling of positive emo-

tions in the heart? A backdoor approach, surely, but one being proven scientifi-
cally in the lab. Institute of HeartMath research has also shown that sustained
positive emotions improve heart rate variability and the efficiency of the elec-
trical signals the heart sends to the brain. Studies show that feelings of care,
joy, appreciation, or love enhance the production of IgA, an immune antibody
known to protect against colds and flu.

Some schools have caught on to the importance of positive emotions. They
are finding that making "care between teachers and administrators" and "care
between children" a high priority works. Learning accelerates, job satisfaction
increases, and absenteeism is reduced. The question then arises, "Is there an efficient method to enhance mental and emotional balance and to enhance positive emotions in administrators, teachers, and children?" The answer is yes.
HeartMath has outlined three key steps. The first step is to understand the difference between your head and your heart so they work for you in balance and
not at cross-purposes. The second step is to learn how to listen to your heart
intuition. The third step is to follow your heart—act on what your heart intuition is saying. These three steps activate a feeling of joy and peace, and accelerate learning. Let's look at each step.

Step 1: Understanding the Difference
Between Your Head and Your Heart

Too many head thoughts, without the balance of heart intuition, generate
rationalizations, overanalysis, self-judgment, anxiety, and many other attitudes
that block real learning. Head thoughts tend to run in a loop, generate negative
emotional reactions, and are hard to shut off. For example, let's say you are a
dedicated teacher overwhelmed with all you have to do. A student comes to
school and didn't do his homework for the umpteenth time. Your head thoughts
automatically kick into gear with judgment. You've given him a lot of time already, taking away from the rest of the class. You think of all the times he's
done this. Resentment builds. He obviously doesn't care or he'd act differently.
Anger rises. The negative emotional reaction fuels the loop. You work long

hours of overtime trying to be a good teacher, and so many kids and parents don't care. Self-pity sets in. The head loop keeps spinning, draining your emotional and physical energy, creating stress, and taking you far away from the joy of teaching.

Your heart intuition has a bailout if you stop the head reactions and listen to it. Heart intuition can show you a creative way through a situation or help you make peace with what you can't change so you don't get into a negative mental and emotional loop. As you practice stopping head reactions at the onset and shift your focus of attention to your heart for a few moments, you can access another source of intuitive intelligence. By focusing your attention on your heart and *choosing* to activate the feeling of love, care, or appreciation for yourself or another, you balance your emotions and you can hear the voice of your intuitive intelligence. You literally "open your heart" to receiving more information. By listening to your heart intuition you can be surprised at the intelligent solutions you get. Heart intuition feels good to your system and brings the joy of discovery. As you clearly see the difference between your heart and your head, they begin to work together in a creative joint venture that brings more understanding, joy, and satisfaction. In the preceding example, if you had stopped the automatic head thoughts at the start and asked your heart intuition for a solution, it may have told you to take a moment to sit down with the student and make an honest heart connection with him, or talk to his parents, or some other answer that felt intuitively right. You save energy, release stress, keep your immune system in balance, and experience the joy of your own understanding. The bonus is this: You gain self-empowerment instead of feeling like a victim.

Step 2: Learning How to Listen to Your Heart

Learning to access and listen to your heart intuition takes practice. In the beginning, you may wonder, "How do I know if my intuition is telling me the right thing?" The accompanying heart feelings of "ah ha," peace, or joy are like inner biofeedback signals that confirm your intuitive feeling of knowing. If you're unsure, you can always stop and ask yourself again, "Am I listening to my heart, or am I just listening to my head concerns or emotional reactions?" Then, shift your attention back to your heart feelings, still the mind a moment, and listen again. A feeling of "knowingness" and a new perception of the situation arises as your mind can now give you an intuitive readout of your heart promptings. After a few days' practice, you gain more power to contact your heart quickly and build more confidence in your intuitive intelligence. Often your solutions may seem very simple. Don't let simplicity fool you. Genius is often hidden behind simplicity. Most people wait until something serious happens before they are forced to go deep in the heart for some answers. Our educational systems have never systematically taught people how to use the heart as a source of intelligence and power. When they do, watch the joy of learning and teaching unfold.

Step 3: Following Your Heart

Many people hear the promptings of their hearts but don't follow them. Following your heart takes courage. But as you practice on simple everyday issues, you build the confidence and self-security to follow your heart on bigger issues. Each time you follow your heart directives and see situations improve as a result, you build more inner security and confidence. Many times, people know what that voice in their heart is telling them, but are afraid to act on it— afraid to speak the truth, afraid of what others will think of them, afraid to ask a question, or simply afraid of the unknown. You can build self-security and courage step-by-step by playing the heart and head game in decision making at home and at work every day until it becomes automatic. The reward is in seeing the quality of your decisions and the quality of your life improve.

Heart management of your day-to-day mental and emotional reactions gets you off the burnout merry-go-round and builds self-empowerment. Let's look at another typical example where heart management can save you much energy and frustration. You are driving to work and you're running late. There's a traffic jam, and cars are inching along at five miles per hour. Your head thoughts kick in, and you start to worry about what the principal might say if you're late again. You get irritated and honk the horn at the lady who just cut in front of you. Your heart is telling you, "Relax, there's nothing you can do anyway until traffic starts moving again."

Your head comes in and says, "I've got too much to do, and that lady's got no business cutting in. Who does she think she is? The city administrators were supposed to widen this road and haven't; they waste taxpayers' money," and on and on. Your irritation turns to frustration. Suddenly your car stalls, and the traffic light turns red again. Anger rises as you pound the steering wheel and swear under your breath. In addition to being emotionally upset, you are releasing stress hormones into your body, which science has already proven accelerate disease and aging. When you get to work, you're so stressed out you don't even notice or care about the child who put a beautiful vase of flowers on your desk. If you had listened to and followed your heart intuition in the first place, you would have saved all that wear and tear. Instead, you could have used your time to relax, appreciated that you had some extra time to plan your day, and kept your heart open to warmly respond to the child who cared about you.

Imagine a school with a staff of 45. If you add up all the fears, irritations, aggravations, backbiting, and other mismanagement of the mental and emotional inner experience of that staff for one day, one week, or one year, you would see a huge energy leak draining the vitality and creativity right out of people. Now imagine this staff becoming mentally and emotionally balanced and self-managed from the heart. Think of how much more joy, vitality, and creativity they would have to spend on teaching and understanding children's needs.

The more you practice following your heart, the more you access powerful energy accumulators that make any job more fun, regenerating, and rewarding. The more you see how heart directives conveniently work for you, the more you come to *trust* them. As you practice, the voice of your heart becomes louder and clearer. The heart intuition helps you make quick on-the-spot mental and emotional attitude adjustments that save you time as well as energy.

You find yourself experiencing more fun and quality—more love, joy, and appreciation of the good things in your life. Heart management of your attitudes and reactions allows the head and heart to work creatively together to bring balance and fulfillment.

Again, the process is simple but takes practice. When you feel stress or find yourself in the middle of a head reaction, simply tell yourself the Heart-Math access code: *Freeze-Frame*—just like pushing the pause button on a VCR. Quiet your mind and emotions, and shift your focus to your heart. This shift helps you to stop identifying with the reaction and gain objectivity. Send out a feeling of love, care, compassion, or appreciation for yourself or another—such activity will open and activate your heart. Then ask your heart intuition, "What would be the most efficient response to this situation?" Pause and listen. Your heart intuition will give your head a creative answer. Remember: Feeling + Perception = Understanding. Understanding brings joy and builds self-empowerment. Heart management simply means going back to the heart for redirection in the middle of any challenge. Heart management can alter the course of events for the rest of your day, or even for the rest of your life.

Deborah Rozman is a businesswoman, psychologist, and author. As Executive Director of the Institute of HeartMath, she is instrumental in developing training programs based on innovative research showing the heart as an information processing system and a central source of intelligence within the human system. She currently conducts workshops and trains trainers in the IHM programs, focusing on heart intelligence as it applies to intuitional development, business, women's issues, parenting, personal effectiveness, and empowerment. Rozman is a contributing editor for some of the Institute's books: Freeze-Frame, A Parenting Manual, *and* Teaching Children to Love, *by Doc Lew Childre, IHM President.*

Every school and every institution communicates values. Sometimes the values are clear. Sometimes the values are less than clear. Sometimes an absence of values is communicated. Sid Simon reflects on his history with values clarification.

16

Joy in Valuing

BY SIDNEY B. SIMON

Values clarification has been the centerpin and the joy of my professional life for almost 40 years. I learned values clarification from Louis Raths, my teacher at New York University, in the mid-'50s. Raths lived and breathed values clarification, and his fire and passion affected almost every one of his graduate students. I remember vividly the very first values clarification lesson Raths taught us.

It's World Series time, circa 1955. We're in New York City, and passions are running high. The Brooklyn Dodgers are matched against the New York Yankees. Raths poses these questions to all of us: "Which team in all of baseball is your favorite team? And which team do you hate the most?" We dutifully wrote those "values" down, and in a small group, we discussed them briefly.

Incidentally, 40 years ago, students didn't normally work in small groups to discuss things, but in Raths's classes you did.

After the small-group discussion, Raths asked the zinger question: "If all the members on the team you love were traded to the team you hate and you got all of *their* players, which team do you *now* root for?" I will never forget the wild and wooly discussions that followed, and how values issues of loyalty, love, hate, circumstance, patriotism, how we've been programmed to think, and at least a dozen other values were explored, challenged, and ultimately clarified.

And week after week in Raths's classes we learned the intricate process called values clarification. Over the 40 years I have plied that subtle craft, I believe thousands of students, and even more participants in our workshops, and maybe a million readers of our books, have benefitted from the joyous values clarification work that Raths started.

Let me tell you about just one small but vivid example of what that values clarification joy looked like. From 1954 to 1957, I taught 10th grade core curriculum at the New Lincoln School in New York City. It was a private progressive school, maybe the liveliest place I have ever taught in, and values clarification was at the heart of all that I taught.

Each year at New Lincoln, my 10th grade class took a week-long field trip to Washington, D.C. Our core theme was politics and government, so we organized a field trip to see our national government close up.

Our trip began with some crucial decision making, decisions made from a values clarification perspective. First, we made the decision that *I* would not make one phone call or write one letter. If phone calls were to be made, students would make them. If letters were to be written, students would write them.

The second decision was also worked out with the class. We would do all the planning as a class. We would break down into small planning committees; each would tackle the variety of problems that had to be faced. We must have spent a full week brainstorming all the problems, chores, and experiences that a trip of this scope entails. We considered little things. Where do we stay? How do we get there? Where does the money come from? What about sex? And discipline? Alcohol and privacy? The list had well over a hundred items. I made sure it contained student time in the Senate Gallery, visits to our congressperson, committee hearings, interviews of lobbyists, and visits to the shrines of our democracy, as well as to the Phillips Art Gallery, the Smithsonian, and Arlington National Cemetery. We even negotiated a social event with an all-black high school class, a pretty radical event in the mid-'50s.

Do you have any idea about how many values issues came up in that planning process? (I remember one sticky one: Should the rich kids be allowed to bring along as much spending money as they wanted? Was that what freedom of choice is about?) As the issues came up, every member in that class learned the values clarification process. They also learned how to fight for that incredibly powerful idea that the majority rules, of course, but that the majority also has a responsibility to consider the objections of the minority and meet them in some way. Democracy is more than just counting votes. It involves negotiation, compromise, and compassion. Merely for your side to win is not enough. Instead, you commit to working long enough so everyone wins.

Those three years of week-long field trips to Washington, D.C., totally planned and carried out by the students themselves, are among the greatest joys in my 40 years of teaching.

But there is one more part of those joyous New Lincoln years to tell you about. Each year, when we got back from the trip, after the journals were shared, letters of thanks written, and summary reports delivered, we had the task of doing our annual 10th grade assembly for the whole school.

For some classes, the assembly was a play, the ubiquitous senior play, a chorus program, or the staging of a town meeting debate. For us, it was always a variety show, with one most fascinating difference: *Every* student in the class committed to being on stage, in some way. In my value system, if we had a class assembly, then the whole class would be involved, not just the 20 best singers or the 6 best actors.

So, once again the class broke itself down into small units, and each unit produced its piece of the revue. We had dramatic scenes from important plays.

We had comedy sketches, sometimes brilliant satires, musical presentations, shadow plays, pantomimes, and poetry read to modern dance. Our variety shows were always long on variety.

But we had another values dimension as well. *Everyone* learned how to work the lights, and everyone learned how and when to pull the curtain. We all pitched in to produce the printed program, the costumes, and the makeup. One of my most joyous moments was to see someone who had just done an exquisite dance piece bow to thunderous applause and then dash to the balcony to relieve "her light man" because his skit was on two slots down on the program. When he was done, he pulled the curtain to open the next act. So it went.

We always ended with a grand finale, with the whole class on stage at one time. The finale was usually a musical item, with new words teasingly written to some popular song and staged so whoever was working lights would set the lights and race back down out of the balcony in time to be in the finale.

We all triumphed. Everyone had a place. Sure, some had more of a triumph, but often because they risked more, not that they necessarily had more talent. Isn't that a value worth teaching?

I have lost touch with most of those students from 40 years ago. The school merged and then, finally and sadly, was closed. But I know wherever they are, those New Lincoln School students will remember what we did. Washington, I bet, will always have a place in their consciousness and in their values. I bet, too, that whenever they go to the theater, a little corner of their psychic memory holds the vision of a 10th grade assembly, where the light-person arrives breathless but proud to take part in a tumultuous finale.

Thanks, Louis Raths. Thanks from the bottom of my heart for values clarification and for the joy it brought to my teaching.

Sidney Simon is an internationally known pioneer in psychological education. He has just retired from teaching, after 40 years on the firing line. For the past 20 years, he has taught at the University of Massachusetts in Amherst. Simon continues to conduct workshops throughout the United States, Canada, Mexico, and Europe. He is one of the authors of the four classic books in values

clarification: Values and Teaching, Values Clarification, Clarifying Values Through Subject Matter, *and* Meeting Yourself Halfway.

    Simon's most recent book is Forgiveness: How to Make Peace with Your Past and Get on with Your Life, *coauthored with Suzanne Simon.*

Once in a while, we have a special day when the perspective that we occasionally lose comes dancing back to us. This was such a day.

17

Downhill Skiing

BY ROBERT SORNSON

It was a jewel of a day. The blue sky and winter sun reflected sharply off the snow. Mountains of snow. Thirty inches had fallen over the past 10 days, but today the storms had gone, leaving the land covered with sparkling, soft powder.

I was riding the chairlift toward the top of Boyne Mountain. Tall Bob was riding in the chair next to me, and down below, I could see Tami, Mark, Tommy Lee, and Dawn, each with their own instructor from the Challenge Ski School. At the top of the hill, waiting to come down, was Matt. His gray jacket, the one he always wore even in school, was half zipped. Matt never got cold. He wore no hat, and his mittens were more holes than cloth. His hair fell down across his eyes, making me wonder how he could possibly see. As we came toward him, he looked up at us and smiled a smile the angels would envy. Matt was in heaven.

I watched as Matt and his instructor started down the hill. Matt took the lead and began a careful traverse, with clean snowplow turns. His style and form looked good. I hadn't thought much about Matt lately. He hadn't been much of a problem, and the nature of my job often seems to be the handling of problems, crises, and blowups. These ski days weren't just good for the students; they also helped me gain perspective and recharge my energies.

My first real introduction to Matt had been in my gym class last year. The records showed that he was mildly retarded, from a poor home, and subject to behavioral outbursts. In the first weeks of school, Matt appeared fearful, quiet, and very nervous. Then one day on the football field, I witnessed what I had only previously heard about. Matt exploded! Someone had been teasing him, and Matt began crying and screaming terrible threats and obscenities. He was louder than a bull moose during mating season. This roaring, angry young man on the field was the Matt of middle school legend. I was amazed, and a little amused.

All attempts to quiet Matt failed. I explained that his behavior was inappropriate and unacceptable. He would have to behave like a gentleman around me. He got quiet for about two seconds then launched into a second tirade. I took him off the field and told him he could rejoin us when, and if, he could get himself under control. It wasn't until the next day that Matt said he was ready to rejoin us. That's the only tantrum he ever had in high school, but not the end of the story.

Matt had a few other characteristics that interfered with his getting along in high school. He was very fat, his clothes smelled, and the noise he most often made was a high, wheedling suck-air sort of giggle. I hate to admit it, but this sound made my scalp tingle and my spine crawl. If I asked him how he was feeling in the morning, he replied with this incredible noise. His reply to most questions was similar. When he did talk, it was in a high squeaky voice, with no volume control. Matt spoke so loudly that most people assumed he was hearing impaired, although tests had shown his hearing was normal.

Every day, we worked on breath and volume control, and gradually Matt's speaking voice improved. We bought him some new clothes, and he began to take better care of himself. Working with me for reading and with another instructor for math, Matt began to improve his 2nd grade level academic skills. He seemed to truly enjoy learning, and he worked hard. In gym class, he could

run more than one lap without dying. He never complained. The slow process of growth seemed to have begun.

The first time we took Matt on a downhill skiing trip he was afraid. Although we live in one of the finest areas in the Midwest for skiing, most of our special students had never tried to ski. It looks so fast, frightening, and formidable. On that first trip, I had Matt and five other students. I made sure Matt had a good instructor and left him in capable hands. By afternoon, he was off the bunny hill and onto the real slopes. His eyes were as alive as I had ever seen them. He fell about 100 times, but he was as proud of that first ski experience as a soldier is proud of his medals.

Matt went downhilling several times last year, learned cross-country skiing in gym class, and was doing well. My focus had moved on to other kids with more pressing problems, and I was stunned when I realized Matt had stopped coming to school in late April. I could hardly believe it when one of the other kids sheepishly reported that Matt was not sick. He was 16.

When I called his home, I was angry and frustrated. In addition to my concern for Matt, I must admit my own ego was involved. Couldn't he see, couldn't his parents understand how important it was for Matt to continue school? I had worked too hard with this kid, and I didn't want to see him go down the tubes. I tried to be composed and professional on the telephone.

"He's quit," his mother told me.

"But he needs to be in school. He's begun to do so well. I really believe he likes school."

"Well," his mother said, "I told him he should go to school, but he's hard to get up in the morning and I can't make him do nothin' these days. His father and I told him he should go. We know he should 'cause we never finished, and we know you can't get no good jobs. But you know his father don't work either 'cause of his back. He just sits home drinking most days. He won't do nothin' with the boy. Just leaves it to me, and I try, but he's too big for me now. Why he just won't listen to . . . ."

It went on like this for some time. Finally I interrupted, "Is Matt there, may I talk to him?" When he came to the phone he sounded embarrassed. After listening to me awhile, Matt said he would come to school the next day, but he didn't.

I called his home again, and this time the person answering sounded just like Matt, but something was wrong. The voice control and the breath control were gone. It was like the old Matt. The high voice shouted at me through the telephone wires. It was Matt's father.

"Matt's not here," he screamed.

"Could I talk to you about Matt coming back to school?" I asked.

"Matt's not here. He's out shopping with his mother," he shouted, so loudly that I had to hold the receiver about four inches away from my ear.

"He needs to be in school," I said. "Do you know how well he's begun doing?"

"His mother's not here."

"Can you bring Matt into school tomorrow so we can sit down and talk about this?" I implored.

"His mother's not here."

"I know she isn't," I replied. "I want you to bring Matt to school to talk."

"Matt quit!" he shouted. I pointed out that Matt was only 16 and couldn't quit without his parents' permission, but to no avail. In the end, Matt's father simply hung up. I could feel the blood rush past my ears toward the top of my head. The conversation had left me furious and shaken. I knew one thing for certain: Matt did not have to turn out like that. He needed to be in school. He needed a chance to learn. A rush of thoughts filled me, quick rationalizations for my feelings. I didn't know this man, but I was angry at him for not caring about his son and for hanging up on me.

While it was against my professional training, and all common sense, I picked up the phone again. Matt's father answered, and I identified myself and told him why I was calling him back.

"I can't talk now," shouted the loudest voice I'd ever heard.

"Do you mean you can't talk or you won't? All you need to do is get Matt up and out of the house in the morning," I said, in my best professional manner.

"I can't talk now," his loud voice cracked and shook.

"Don't you want to see—"

He hung up on me—again.

Now my emotions were way out of hand. I am ashamed to admit that I called him back a third time. I'm not sure which of us was louder, but it was a very short conversation, and Matt's father hung up again. I felt lousy. I was ashamed for losing my temper and saddened by the thought of losing Matt. My pride was hurt: I was proud that our program had so few dropouts.

Matt didn't return to school that year. But when the new school year began in the fall, Matt was there. He worked hard and it only took us a couple of weeks to get his voice back under control. He had gained a few pounds but worked steadily in PE, and by winter, he was looking better than I had ever seen. His giggle was gone. He no longer squirmed constantly when sitting. He could look you straight in the eye and smile. A couple of times, I saw him stand up for himself without losing control of his temper. Matt was learning more each new day.

Now, as I watched him racing downhill on his skis, with grace, skill, and confidence, I felt glad for Matt, knowing that while he still had a long way to go, he had come a very long way already.

Surrounded by beautiful hills, pines, and unending hardwood forests, skiing offered Matt a significant challenge. Yet there is an allure to downhill skiing: the grace, the balance, the individual responsibility, the white silence, and the camaraderie of meeting challenge among friends. At the end of the day, thanks to our good instructors, there is a strong sense of accomplishment and pride.

The chairlift reached the summit, and Tall Bob and I raised the tips of our skis to get off. Tall Bob was nervous. We'd been on the bunny hill most of the morning, learning to balance, snowplow, and turn. He was still stiff and tight and almost knocked me over getting out of the chair. I enjoyed working with Tall Bob. Nervous as he was, and as many times as he fell, he kept smiling, trying, and enjoying. He gave off a pleasant, energetic glow that made me feel good each time he did a little better.

Late in the day, I found myself riding alone in the chairlift. Most of my students were skiing in a group. The early dusk of winter began to reach its long finger shadows across the white slopes of Boyne Mountain. Matt, with his unzipped coat, traversed smoothly down the slope. Tall Bob yelled across the hill to him. Mark shot past them both, still the hotdog. Tami and Dawn skied together, following each other's tracks. Tommy Lee followed at a distance.

No one really knows what makes a kid move toward health and strength. Maybe a summer of growing or a surge of hormones can do more than any of us teachers. Modeling healthy adults seems to help some kids, especially adults who believe that self-defeating behaviors can be left behind and who offer kids a chance to grow and experience themselves as winners.

Bob Sornson is coeditor of this book and a special education teacher turned administrator. Intensely interested in everything under the sun (and the moon and the stars), Sornson has a special interest in the incredible diversity of thinking and learning styles of children and adults, and for the potential in each human being.

Where did you model the basic habits of character that have carried you forward in your life? Lois Wolfe-Morgan tells her story.

18

Meet My First Mentor

BY LOIS WOLFE-MORGAN

One of the most powerful influences in my life has been my father, Larry Lyden. He has been a mentor to me all of my life in many ways. He's approaching 87 years of age, but you would never know it to look at him. He's a lively gentleman who is constantly whistling. He has never lost the bounce in his step and the "snap" in his personality.

He's very firm in his beliefs. He's not without his weaknesses. He is an alcoholic. He has great strengths, and he has been sober for more than two decades. But regardless of his state of sobriety, he has always been one of the most caring and loving people I have ever known. There has been a strong bond between us for as long as I can remember. Although I was one of eight children, Dad always had a way of making me feel special. I can remember him cuddling me as a child, making me laugh when I was sad, and above all, treating me like I was special and not just another mouth that needed to be fed.

Source: Adapted by permission of Knowledge, Ideas, and Trends, Inc., Manchester, Conn., from *Build Your Own Road* by Lois Wolfe-Morgan. Copyright © 1997 by Lois Wolfe-Morgan.

Teaching & Joy

Dad instilled in me some powerful life insights. He has never done anything "by the book." He has built his own road his own way, and he has enjoyed his successes. He's not a wealthy man. In fact, Dad and Mom live off social security and the income generated from a lawn-mower repair business he operates out of his garage. Yet, he is wealthy in many ways. He's never lost his determination to enjoy life. And each time something positive has happened in my life, Dad has been on hand to cheer me on, always reminding me how proud he is of me.

I have always taken my problems to Dad. He has always told me, "Lois, I can't solve your problems, but you can talk with me about them." Many times, I have found that talking out my problems revealed a solution. Dad always looks on the good side of every situation, and he taught me how to do that early in life. Just that ability alone has helped me weather a lot of stormy situations.

Dad isn't well educated in the academic sense. In fact, he jokes that he was kicked out of the 3rd grade because he wouldn't shave. Yet, he has taught me things I never learned in school, or even college, for that matter. For starters, he taught me that love of self and other people is essential to getting through life with any semblance of sanity. And watching him live his beliefs has shown me that loving others is a lot more fun—and productive—than living a life full of hate, bitterness, and resentment.

Dad taught me about building roads

Most important, Dad was the person who taught me the importance of building my road into the future. I learned that at the tender age of 4, when I worked my first "job" as a milkman. Actually, Dad was the milkman—the best milkman in the territory. That's what he told me, and that's what I believed.

I don't remember the exact day I began working the milk route with Dad, but I do remember some of the adventures we had. I wore bib overalls—just like Dad's, except mine were made of corduroy. They were our uniforms. Dad started his route at 4:30 a.m. Three hours later, he'd swing by our house and pick me up. Every night when I went to bed, I looked forward to the next morning with eager anticipation, because I loved riding on the milk truck, and I simply adored my dad.

104

Since I was very tiny in stature, Dad built a seat for me out of two milk crates and positioned it on the passenger side of the truck. He tied a rope through the handles so I wouldn't tumble about. But best of all was that he made the seat high enough for me to see outside. We made our daily rounds, singing songs, learning words from signs and billboards, and talking to customers and laughing. We were very good at laughing.

At times, the roads were rough. Michigan winters are known for their destruction of unpaved streets. Some of the roads annoyed me because they caused the milk bottles to clink and my teeth to gnash.

One day, I asked Dad, "Why doesn't somebody fix this road?"

He said, "Sometimes, we have to travel rough roads. If it's important enough for you to get where you're going, then you won't mind traveling a rough road and making the best of it." Then he'd say something to make me laugh, and I'd forget about all the bumps and the jolts.

On another day, Dad decided that one of the roads was simply too rough for the truck to handle, so he detoured on another road that we didn't usually take.

"No, no!" I yelled. "Daddy, we've got to go to the next road!"

Dad just smiled. "Sometimes, if a road is too rough to ride, we simply have to take another road."

Of course, I didn't immediately perceive the significance of these lessons. But as I got older, I understood how they applied to our lives. Sometimes, the roads leading to our destinations are rough. We can either choose to forget about going where we want, or we can do our best to cope with the rough road. And if our vision of self-defined success is important enough for us to achieve, we won't mind taking the rough roads.

But sometimes if a road is simply too rough for travel, we can find an alternate route. For example, I would have preferred going to college for four years immediately after graduation from high school. Lack of money ruled out that option. But Dad always told me, "If you can't get what you want one way, find another way to get it." I found another road. It was a long one, and even that road was rough at times. It took me 25 years of night classes to earn a master's degree. But I finally achieved the goal because I was willing to take the road leading to it.

I could go on forever about the lessons I've learned from Dad. But one of the most recent lessons that has helped guide me as a speaker, trainer, and business owner involves his work as a lawn-mower repairman.

Dad bought a broken-down lawn mower from his neighbor for $10. The mower was in such poor shape that the neighbor felt lucky to get $10 for it. Dad immediately went to work on the machine. He invested a lot of time and effort into restoring it to practically mint condition. Then he sold the lawn mower for $180—to the neighbor who had sold it to him for $10.

At first, the neighbor didn't recognize the mower. He was so impressed with the way it appeared and the sound of its engine that it never crossed his mind it could be the same machine. Dad made sure that his neighbor knew he was buying back his original lawn mower. But the neighbor didn't mind paying 18 times as much as he'd received for it to buy it back, because he felt Dad's effort had made it worth that amount.

The same principle works with human beings. No matter what you think you're worth, you can increase your actual value to yourself and others—if you're willing to put in the time and effort.

Lois Wolfe-Morgan travels internationally, presenting seminars on such topics as managing negativity, self-directed leadership, stress and fatigue intervention, interpersonal communications skills, self-esteem building, secretarial development, supervisory development, and customer service. She sponsors "POWER-UP Breakfasts and Conferences for Women."

Wolfe-Morgan began her 19-year career with the federal government as a file clerk. In the course of her evolution, she became Program Director for Executive and Managerial Development.

Some moments will stay with us forever. Taken collectively, these moments of learning and joy are the fabric of our culture.

19

Impact

BY GUY VANDER JAGT

Johnny's father gave 6-year-old Johnny a jigsaw puzzle map of the United States for Christmas. He explained to Johnny, "I am going to mix up the pieces, and it's going to be hard for you to put them together because you've never studied geography. When you get stuck, just bring me the puzzle and I'll help you get started again. If you stay with it, in a few months, I guarantee you will have the jigsaw puzzle map finished, and you will have learned a lot about the United States."

Johnny loved presents. After his dad mixed up the pieces, shaking the box real hard, he gave it to Johnny. Twenty-two minutes later, the little boy came running back into his father's den, carrying the completed jigsaw puzzle map of the United States. His father was astounded and ready to think he may have a genius on his hands. "How did you do it, Johnny? Did you get someone to help you?"

"No," Johnny answered, "no one helped me. It was easy, Dad. On the other side of the map there is a picture of a man. All you have to do is put the man together right, and the United States comes out right, too!"

Teaching & Joy

Educators engage in the business of helping people put themselves together, and if we do it right, our nation will be all right, too. In the face of seemingly overwhelming complexities aimed at us daily from the local, city, county, state, and federal bureaucracies, plus the ever-present communications media, educators must hold tightly to their ideals, nurture the belief that the most important person in the educational process is the student, and remember our individual impact on each student in the classroom. Our mannerisms, facial expressions, vocal tones, and hygiene habits all must be considered daily, right alongside our lesson plans.

Teachers usually have a treasure trove of special stories that highlight the impact they have had upon individual students. I have one about a teacher I never had the privilege of meeting, but I have certainly known many of her spiritual brothers and sisters in the teaching profession.

A few years ago, one of George Canter's syndicated news columns in the *Detroit News* caught my attention. Mr. Canter had taken issue with his own newspaper over an obituary he had seen the previous day. It read, "Louise Beck, Retired Teacher, No Survivors."

Mr. Canter wrote a vehement denial to that obituary. He had never known Miss Beck's first name, but he certainly knew who she was—the English teacher 26 years ago who had inspired him to write. It wasn't any specific thing she said or did, but the impact of her positive attitude and overall personality at a vulnerable time in his life that left an indelible memory. "I know one survivor at least," he wrote, "a columnist for the *Detroit News*." As long as Miss Beck survives in Mr. Canter's memory, the phrase "no survivors" doesn't apply.

That column started me thinking about my own 4th grade teacher, whom I will refer to as Miss King. She made a tremendous impact on me and, I bet, on the rest of my class many years ago. I cannot recall any specific thing she said or did that was different from other teachers. Yet, I remember the 4th grade as my happiest learning experience—a warm, sunny room, and a caring teacher. Miss King cared about her subject matter *almost* as much as she cared about helping her students learn.

Many years later, I learned that Miss King had been diagnosed with an incurable illness the same year I was experiencing the joy of learning in her classroom. She had only a short time to live, and being a maiden lady of indeterminable age without family ties, she had been able to create a comfortable nest egg.

Miss King told her fellow teachers (one of whom would later tell me this story) that she was going to Europe to see all the places she had always dreamed and taught about. Her colleagues were happy for her and eager to do what they could to speed her on her journey. The school principal had told her she could begin planning and packing immediately and would not have to return to school. Imagine his surprise the following day when he walked by her classroom to check on the substitute's progress—Miss King was leaning against the window sill, in the middle of the classroom, supervising an impromptu spelling bee. When he asked her what she was doing there, she answered, "I can't leave my students in the middle of the year. They need me." Miss King never made it to Europe. I can attest, however, that when Miss King departed this world, she left many survivors.

Do any of us educators really understand the enormity of our power as we stand in front of our students? We affect tomorrow's generation not so much through our transmission of knowledge but through the force of our personalities. Does a greater joy exist than making a positive impact on another human being? With our captive audience, we teachers have a new opportunity every day to reassure students that they are special; inspire them to work to their potential; help them to realize their value; offer them another perspective; and instill within each a love of learning for its own sake. I never learned any of these things in college. I don't think they can be taught. They must simply be lived, so that others may learn through their impact.

Guy Vander Jagt began his public career as a teacher and minister at a small church in Tustin, Michigan. He was first elected to the United States Congress from Michigan in 1966 and served for nearly 28 years, until January 1993. In the House of Representatives, he became the second ranking

Republican on the Ways and Means Committee and the ranking Republican on the House Trade Subcommittee, the Select Revenue Measures Subcommittee, and the Health and Human Resources Subcommittee. He also served as a member of the Joint Taxation Committee.

In addition to his legislative duties, Congressman Vander Jagt served for nearly two decades as Chairman of the National Republican Congressional Committee, making him the top political and campaign leader for Republicans in the House of Representatives. He served as a national chairman longer than any person of either political party in U.S. history. He currently serves as counsel to the national law firm of Baker and Hostetler in Washington, D.C.

Valla Dana Fotiades is a joyous being with a recipe that won't go wrong!

20

Ignite the Joy Within!

BY VALLA DANA FOTIADES

As a former elementary school teacher, I would like to share some ideas that will help ignite the "joyful sparks" in your students. These ideas will help you focus on the moments, thoughts, actions, and accomplishments that bring joy to our own lives and to one another daily.

1. Joy Journal

End the summer and ring in the fall with each student starting a Joy Journal. Make the first entry capture the joyful memories of summer. Thereafter, students note positive accomplishments, happy moments, thoughtful comments, and nurturing compliments, and record them in their Joy Journals. Do this daily, weekly, or at random. Only—and I repeat, only—wonderful, joyful things enter the pages of this journal. You may wish to save this journal and look through it to give you a boost during any downtimes. The Joy Journal may also be shared with your family. It will let others know what makes you sparkle and permeates your pores with joy. The Joy Journal also helps you counterbalance your thoughts and focus on the positives in a world that has a tremendous amount of sadness and fear.

Teaching & Joy

2. Who Are You?

May I introduce you? This is a great first-day icebreaker. Have students pair up with someone they do not know too well, or better yet, someone who is a total stranger. Each student works with an $8\frac{1}{2}$" x 11" sheet of paper and brightly colored marking pens. Partner A speaks while Partner B creates a name tag for Partner A. Partner A tells Partner B five to seven proud accomplishments. Students should avoid using roles (e.g., I am a good sister). Partner B writes Partner A's name in the middle of the sheet and jots brief notes on the positive accomplishments around the name to create the name tag. After Partner A's name tag is complete, reverse roles. When all name tags are complete, people introduce their partners to the class by giving the name first and then summarizing the accomplishments. Clap after each introduction for all the wonderful achievements.

This exercise is conducive to developing new friendships, encouraging communication, and best of all, building self-esteem. Store this name tag in the T/A envelope (see Idea 3).

3. Talent/Accomplishment Tree

Create a Talent/Accomplishment Tree—use a bulletin board all year to be the "T/A Tree." (That takes care of one of those fun bulletin boards, teachers!) Each student creates an envelope with a list of talents and accomplishments. The envelopes are attached to the bulletin board and can be added to at any time throughout the year.

4. Goals Work

Working hand in hand with the T/A Tree, ask each student to create a Goal Book for the year. Break goals into such categories as educational, emotional, physical, and social. You decide what categories work best and how many to concentrate on. An example is a goal in the educational category—Step 1: Student sets a goal to read 30 books this year; Step 2: Student writes down the goal

and the individual steps needed to make it happen (e.g., read three books each month); Step 3: Student records the goal and steps to make it happen on 3" x 5" cards; Step 4: Student checks off the accomplishment when completed and pops it into the T/A Tree envelope.

A teacher might also give special weekly awards to students who are most helpful, kind, observant, diligent, creative, and patient. These awards could go into the T/A Tree envelope. You could even have the children develop the parameters for the award as well as the selection process and then vote (secret ballot) to select weekly winners.

5. Be Human

Build bridges of "humanness" with the students. Devote a segment of time for a "Be Human" discussion that could include values; what makes me joyful; where and when am I most creative; when do I feel most useful; what kinds of things frighten me; my most embarrassing moment; what makes me sad; my favorite season; what is *my* purpose here on earth; and when, where, and with whom am I most happy.

My class held this discussion for 30 minutes during the last period on Fridays when kids and the instructor can be relaxed. What a super way to end the week and create the desire for kids to return to school on Monday.

Perhaps some students, with input from the teacher, might come up with the weekly topics. This particular strategy helps all of us to understand diversity in thoughts and also to realize that having different opinions and ideas is not only okay and healthy but makes life interesting.

I have found that if the group sits in a circle, a nice, warm, bonding, communicative atmosphere is created. I use a Koosh ball (you can find one in a toy shop) to select who speaks. Only the Koosh holder is allowed to talk; the one exception is the group leader, who needs to keep the group on target. "Be Human" discussions are a good opportunity for students and teachers to share the leadership role.

6. Humor and Health

Inject humor into daily life. As humorist Rosemary Verri says, "Practice inverse paranoia—pretend everyone in the world is out to make you happy and look for the humor in life. It's everywhere!"

Humor has such a positive effect on our immune system. Teach kids to smile often. Practice by teaching them what I call the Tonsil Smile—smile *so big* I can see your tonsils. How about an Alligator Smile? Show *all* those teeth! Hang a mirror close by so everyone can check on their progress.

7. Wing Practice

While you have them smiling, how about teaching Wing Practice together with Wing Walking? Everyone stands up and tries to pull their wings (shoulder blades) toward their spine. We get energized, refreshed, great posture, and a laugh! What could be more healthy? It takes only a moment, practices excellent posture in a fun and joking spirit, and boosts energy. Next time your students appear a little bent over, are yawning and sleepy, try it, you'll like it! Wing Walking is also fun when a line of students walks in the hall. (Mothers from my workshops tell me they love the Wing Practice technique.)

8. On Your Feet—Speak!

Diminish the fear of public speaking. Start the morning, the afternoon, or after a recess with an impromptu speech. Have a topic box where students can suggest topics. Spend one to two minutes a student or choose two students each day. This activity is a great focus technique—everyone will want to hear what the speaker has to say—it sparks creative thinking and builds confidence; promotes consistency in daily rituals; and helps everyone learn to speak "on their feet." The more one practices, the easier public speaking becomes. Clap after each speaker to boost that speaker's self-esteem. Sometimes the teacher must also participate. Sample books for more ideas include *A Whack on the Side of the Head* and *A Kick in the Seat of the Pants* by Roger von Oech.

9. Create a Magic Mission

Create a mission statement. First, students work in pairs and write down each other's answers to these four questions:

1. What is our purpose in our class this year?

2. What is *really* our purpose?

3. What are the qualities we want our class to nurture and inspire in ourselves and others?

4. What steps can we take to help us make our purpose a reality?

When pairs have shared their thoughts, join two pairs together and combine thoughts to answer all questions. Assign a person as the note taker. Write the joint answers on a large poster to display in the classroom. Select a team of three students to combine all the information and create the mission statement for the class. This exercise gives students a feeling of having created the atmosphere they wish, *and* it gives the entire class a strong focus on the class purpose for the year. Evaluate at midyear and revise if necessary.

As a follow-up, ask each student to write a personal mission statement, which works in harmony with the class mission statement. For more information about mission statements, see *The 7 Habits of Highly Effective People* by Dr. Stephen Covey.

10. Dream on

As a child, how many times did you say to yourself, "When I grow up, I'm going to be . . . , do . . . , go . . ."? Give students a chance now and then to "think wild." Inspire them to dream their wildest dreams of who they want to be when they grow up (and right now for that matter), what they want to be, where they would like to travel, whom they would like to meet, and what kinds of things they would like to be remembered for. Write these dreams down. Make dream books that include both written dreams and pictures of the ideas that represent their dreams.

Writing down thoughts and cutting out pictures of what we dream to attain inspires us to determined action. Encourage students to review their lists 20 years from now to see how many dreams became reality—a lot, I'd bet! Store these in the T/A Tree envelopes.

11. When I Can Only See You

The most important thing we wear is our expression. Teach students a little about body language. Think about how we would know a lot about someone's personality even if we could only observe that person from behind a one-way mirror and never hear a word of conversation. Discuss what makes a person appear to be the kind of person we would like to have for a friend. Do we see those qualities in ourselves? Do we want to? Can we work on projecting those qualities?

Have some fun. Take an observation walk occasionally, and analyze who the happy, sad, relaxed, contented, aggravated, uncomfortable, mad, and enthusiastic people are. What do you observe about their posture, gestures, and facial expressions? Role-play and re-create the scenes. Have the students try to feel those emotions and act out the posture, gestures, and facial expressions.

This practice in observation helps us see, feel, and act out what makes people who they are and allows us to gather information and think about characteristics we might like to avoid or emulate. We can then work on projecting our true essence, creating the most comfortable and effective and wonderfully genuine "me" I can be!

12. Smile!

Remember the humor tips in Idea 6? Hang a picture in the classroom of someone sharing a huge smile. It could even be a chimpanzee! Why? Dr. John Diamond, in his book *Your Body Doesn't Lie,* states that smiling helps strengthen the thymus gland, an important contributor to a healthy immune system. He believes that smiling, or even looking at a smile, gives us what he calls "life energy."

How about taping a smiling face on the top corner of every student's desk or even creating a bulletin board packed with smiles. Can I see your tonsils yet?

13. Discover P.Y.P.C.

P.Y.P.C. (Program Your Personal Computer) has to do with attitude, positive thoughts, and actions. Shad Helmstetter, in his book *What to Say When You Talk to Yourself*, relates that "as much as 77 percent of everything we think is negative, counterproductive, and works against us."

From my experience, I firmly believe that if we want to, we can turn around with determination and positive programming. Imagine our potential if we could be programmed with 70 percent to 100 percent positive input. Wow! Unlimited potential! *You* can inspire this positive growth and personal development progress in others.

Have students imagine, visualize, and think about everything they want to do and be. They create their own statements. Write the statements on small self-stick notes. Tell them to post the notes on their bedroom or bathroom mirrors where they can read their statements in the morning and at night. Remind them to tell themselves positives throughout the day.

Do a physical check on programming progress. Start the day with 20 bingo chips in your left pocket, and each time you give yourself or someone else a sincere compliment, transfer a chip to your right pocket. You will see if you are actually living, doing, and speaking in a positive way.

Here are some examples of positive programming: I am intelligent; I am creative; I am patient and kind; I am helpful; I am healthy; I create my opportunities for success; everything I create turns out better than I ever imagined; I am humorous; I am organized; I am calm, relaxed, and having fun; and I love my life and the people in it.

14. Nurture Nature

Nurture the love of nature. Walk in nature with your students. Incorporate a science learning lesson where students take time to smell the flowers, feel the wind blow through their hair, and hear the wind make the leaves dance. Ask them to close their eyes and breathe in the season's scent and experience warm sunshine or wet raindrops on their faces. See if they can search out the cloud animals, and speak and sing with the birds. Take a magnifying glass to thoroughly appreciate the beauty around us—flowers, bugs, leaves, and tree bark. By nurturing the love of nature now, you may trigger a practice in your students that they can enjoy throughout their lives. Use all your senses. Lap up the exuberance! Inhale life!

15. Music, Oh Yes, Music

Capture the ears and hearts of your students by creating a joyful atmosphere with music. Surely you have been captivated by the emotional changes powered by music. Start the day or a break during the day with some fun, enlightening, relaxing, and energizing music. Use music to inspire thoughts and ideas in creative writing class or art. You can create the mood. I play songs from musicals like *The Sound of Music, The Music Man, South Pacific, Oklahoma!,* and *Annie.* Be creative and use your favorites. It's up to you!

16. Challenges

Challenge and be challenged. This idea surfaced from my life experiences over the last two years. I have found myself in the fortunate position of having others believe very strongly in my abilities to achieve. Colleagues have invited (challenged is more accurate) me into leadership roles that I have found to be motivating, energizing, and phenomenal growth experiences. These experiences made me aware of how I frequently challenge others, in a nurturing and positive way, to try something they have not done, to venture into something new, and to take a risk. And to enjoy the personal growth that bursts forth. This practice helps everyone move to a higher level of achievement. Challenge others and at the same time challenge yourself—be a challengee. Look upon challenge with the spirit of an adventurer. Experience abundant and immediate

growth—like Jack's beanstalk. See it, feel it, act it! And as Ethel Cook, creator of internationally celebrated "Do It! Day," emphatically declares, "Just Do It!"

I sincerely hope I have given you some practical ideas for creating joy in your teaching, doing, learning, and living, and for igniting "joyful sparks" in your students. Have a ton of fun, be enthusiastic, love who you are, whom you are with, and what you do:

Dream and teach others to do the same.
Strive to do your best, be your best, and share that best with others.
Enjoy special moments every day even if in a very small way!

Smile a lot—be creative.
It's *so* healthy—you'll see.
And laugh, share emotions—be human—really BE!

Commit your dreams and goals to paper.
Believe in yourself.
Surround yourself with others who believe in you, too.
Add boundless determination.
And take action to make it all come true!

Valla Dana Fotiades is an educator, motivator, author, and TV host. She is a Past President of the New England Speakers Association, a member of the National Speakers Association's Leadership Team, founding President of the Central Massachusetts Esteem Team (a chapter of the National Association for Self-Esteem), founder of International Boost Your Self-Esteem Month (February), and creator of the Joy *Journal.*

Fotiades has been sharing seeds of hope and challenge to inspire our fellow humans even before she began teaching in Canada in 1972. As a professional speaker and workshop leader, she teaches people how to embrace life and energize to excel!

Like spring after winter, sometimes joy must follow sorrow.

21

A Journey of Trust and Joy

BY MARY GAYLE FLODEN

I was sitting at my desk, feeling warm and content, as snow fell gently against the window. The phone rang, and I heard the voice of a former student in a class I taught, Women and Holistic Health.

She was crying and upset: "Mary Gayle, this is Marsha. I'm wondering if you would be willing to see Diane. She just heard she has ovarian cancer, and I don't know what to do to help her. Can you help?"

Diane was a full-time student at our community college and was soon to graduate. She had been in my Women and Holistic Health class several years before, and I remembered her as a lovely young woman, earnest and goal-directed. Now in her early 30s, Diane had cancer. A ripple of disbelief ran through my own body.

"Of course," I heard myself saying, "have her call me. I'd be happy to walk with her on the journey." I hung up the phone and looked out the window, thinking how quickly our lives can change with just a phone call.

The snow was blanketing the yard that day. It looked so peaceful and serene, so completely untouched by human frailty. I can recall my quiet prayer, seeking help and direction as I embarked on this new journey with Diane.

When I shared Diane's plight with my nursing students the next morning, I asked them to be aware of how precious each day is, and to consider how they

might react if they found out they had cancer. How would their lives change? Would they continue with school? We all have a plan. I asked my students to give some thought to their plans but to also think about alternate plans. All of us agreed that life is precious, and we gave thanks to Diane for helping us to remember. She was one of us, part of the whole.

Diane and I saw the winter blanket melt away and the spring flowers bring new hope as she underwent a bone marrow transplant. I saw her every day. We talked, laughed, and sometimes cried together. Diane studied protocols for treatment and read all she could about portacaths and chemotherapeutic agents. The nursing students continued learning more about compassion, commitment, and human suffering. I would share Diane's progress with them, and they would send support and encouragement to both of us.

I was deeply touched by the students' trust and compassion. They trusted me as their teacher and guide. They trusted Diane's process as well as their own. Diane and I walked together on life's path, a path that would become a journey of trust. Through her suffering, courage, and quest for knowledge and acceptance, Diane would become one of my master teachers.

We spent time talking. We saw the seasons change, and our world became focused on numbers and blood counts—all the medical criteria for stability. At the same time, the nursing students were studying the numbers and memorizing nursing diagnoses and outcome criteria.

In February, when the snow returned, Diane and I sat together in my study, preparing to talk as we often did about her process, her life, and now, her death. She had agreed to videotape one of our sessions to help future nursing students know how important they are to those who are suffering. Diane loved her nurses, and her nurses loved her. They had been with her throughout her surgeries, chemotherapy, bone marrow transplant, and now, the final stages of her cancer. Diane trusted them completely. She trusted me and she trusted herself. She wanted to share this gift of trust with the nursing students who had been such a large part of her life during the two years she underwent therapy. The videotape reflects her strength, knowledge, and love of life.

Diane died in the summer when the flowers were in full bloom. The nursing students who walked with her graduated and took the gifts she gave them to a new community.

I sit in my study now, watching the leaves fall to the ground. My yard will soon be again covered in snow. I hear Diane's voice whispering to me, "Go have fun," and I am thankful that I am part of a universal community of colearners—teachers as students, students as teachers. I trust that everyone I meet is my teacher; and I trust that love, compassion, and goodwill are my gifts to share. In sharing, I find joy. And teaching is sharing.

Mary Gayle Floden is a certified psychosynthesis therapist and imagery trainer. She received her Master of Science degree from Northern Illinois University, and is a Professor of Nursing at the College of Dupage in Glen Ellyn, Illinois. She has been involved in designing, coordinating, and teaching educational programs related to holistic health and wellness for more than two decades. Floden serves as a consultant and therapist for Mind/Body Harmony in Glen Ellyn, Illinois. She also has a private practice of individual, family, and group counseling, where she combines a variety of holistic and traditional techniques to suit the individual needs of her clients.

Sometimes teachers help students discover purpose in life. Sometimes,
however, teachers discover their own purpose.

22

Discovering Purpose

BY RICK SCOTT

In my first year as a teacher, I was sure I had learned all I needed to know
about proper classroom procedure. All the students sat in rows at individual
desks. Talking or other disruptions were not allowed while they were working.
If students had questions, they were expected to ask me. After all, I was the expert and if I didn't know the answer, then it wasn't worth knowing. I thought I
was doing my job very well. My students worked, remained quiet, turned in
their assignments, and were generally productive. We moved smoothly from
one unit to the next, and everyone was on the same text chapter in any subject. And yet, I missed all the classic signs of what was really going on in my
classroom that first year.

Looking back, I should have noticed the signs. I remember teaching the
concept of metaphors by presenting the material lecture style, as I always did. I
had learned that way, so it must be the correct way to teach. I finished the pres-
entation and asked for questions. At first, nothing but silence. Then, a tentative
hand from the back of one of the rows.

"Yes?" I asked, hoping for the best.

"I thought a metaphor was someone who fought bulls," one student said.

The other students, much to their credit, did not howl with laughter, and I was pleased with their decorum. Only later did I realize that they were just as confused as the student who spoke up. I patiently explained the whole concept again, in the same lecture style. This time, no one asked questions, and I blindly assumed everyone understood my words.

The following year, I taught a grade 5/6 split gym class. Again, I brought my rigid teaching standards to the task. I was teaching volleyball skills, with the students in groups of four to practice volleying the ball around their respective group. I told the students to pass the ball in a clockwise motion. The first question, of course, was, "Which way is clockwise?"

"You know, it's the way a clock moves," I said, "from 12 to 1 to 2 and so on."

A student replied, "Doesn't it depend on which wall you hang the clock?" I walked away, shaking my head at his ignorance. I had missed a teachable moment altogether. Still, nothing fazed me. I was doing a good job. I was teaching and the kids were quiet.

During my fourth year, things started coming together for me. I was assigned a 6th grade class. We had two reading programs: the Ginn 720 program for the average to above-average readers and Open Highways for those with below-average reading skills. The reading lesson involved getting the Ginn 720 group working independently so I could spend necessary time reading aloud to the Open Highways group.

In those days, the teacher's guide was a big book with metal rings for binding. One day, I had this guide open to the story I was reading in class. I walked around the perimeter of the group, keeping my eye on both the page and the students. They were quiet. I assumed they were listening. As I walked around the room, I started to get bored with the story. So I began to work my thumb up through the metal rings of the guide, all the way to the last knuckle. The students were still listening as I talked. No one appeared to notice that I continued teaching from the book with my thumb firmly stuck in the binding. As our time drew to a close, I began pulling harder, but my thumb just kept getting caught on the metal tab. Desperation set in. What could I do? I remembered the adage from teachers' college: "Never show pain or emotion." I looked at the group I was teaching. No one was paying any attention to my problem. Instead, they were looking toward the ceiling or down at the floor, twiddling their own thumbs. Their books were open, but I saw now that they hadn't been paying attention to a word I was saying the entire time. But, THEY WERE QUIET! This was my first real epiphany.

With only one way to extricate my thumb, I yanked as hard as I could. A long gash appeared down the side of my thumb. Blood started to flow. I quickly left the room, and holding my thumb, I let out a howl of pain before running to the office for a Band-Aid. Returning to my class, I found that the students had no idea why I had left. No one had noticed anything unusual. I knew things had to change.

Now, instead of answers, all I had were questions as I looked for ways and means to involve my students in the learning process. My professional reading increased, along with a sense of mission. In *Learning Magazine*, I found an article about cooperative learning that described a method of grouping students so that they relied on each other for help. After careful study, I was eager to give it a try. When I explained the "new" way of teaching to the students, they agreed to a trial run. Their attitude seemed to be "Anything is better than what we're doing now."

I placed the students in groups as described in the article. I thought we would be back in rows by recess. But the students surprised me. They may even have surprised themselves. They accepted the assigned groups and the learning situation. The noise level rose, but I was warned to expect that. The whole experiment worked tremendously well. The students changed groups from time to time so everyone had a chance to work with everyone else, but we stayed in groups until the end of June. Since then, I have used cooperative learning groups in my classes, even now at the high school level.

Cooperative learning has given me insight into what it means to be student centered and what it means to teach students to care for themselves and for others. I wasn't too sure about getting students to care for others until this past year.

Teaching & Joy

I had to attend meetings in another town for our school district, leaving my class for two weeks. I left a note on the board, telling them I was sorry I couldn't be with them and that I would miss them. I also told them they could write me letters telling me about their days. I received a nice note outlining how the day went and what this particular student did. I received a phone call from another student, asking how I was feeling and if I was all right. I assured her I was fine. In a nervous voice, she assured me that she was all right, too. She said it was important for her to know I was okay.

The next evening, after I had attended another day filled with meetings, my wife answered a knock at the door. A delivery man had flowers for Rick Scott from a group of students, with a card that said "We miss you!" It was then I realized that my purpose in life—teaching—was truly being fulfilled.

My professional reading and studying now includes using cooperative learning in conjunction with quality schools and outcome-based education, always looking for effective ways to teach students the "caring" that is seldom outlined in any of our curriculums, yet is taught daily by joyous teachers everywhere.

Rick Scott has been teaching for 16 years at both the elementary and secondary levels. In 1993, he completed his Master's Degree in Administration and Curriculum. He has published articles on cooperative learning.

23

An Interview with Bernie Siegel, M.D.

BY ROBERT SORNSON

R.S.: What's the connection between great learning and joy?

Bernie: I have come to the realization that you have to be open-minded to learn. The history of man shows that we've sometimes fought new information and new ideas. People have been crucified for saying things like, "The earth is round," or "The earth isn't the center of the universe." There is no joy in that. It ends exploring and learning.

That's why I like to use the word "mystery" when I don't understand something. I can accept, explore, and learn from it. Ignorance comes from nonacceptance.

Sometimes I tell people I'm starting a new religion and the symbols are ice, Band-Aids, and pennies. Ice because it defies the laws of physics by being lighter than water and allowing our planet to survive. A Band-Aid because of how the body heals beneath it without our thinking about it or consciously doing anything. And on the penny it says, "In God We Trust." You have to ultimately rely on the intelligence that began the whole universe, and so you are in awe. I use the word "God" in a liberal way. This intelligent energy, as I call it, loves us and provides us with a lot of interesting phenomena that we need to look at and keep exploring.

Frequently, I talk about following intuitive knowledge. If you look at many of the great changes in our history, they came from individuals who were intuitive, who woke up from a dream, who thought something was different. These are people who were open to new possibilities and to their inner guidance. They did not rely solely on the path of intellect. That doesn't mean that we don't use our intellect or that we stop thinking. Intellect just isn't the whole solution. For me, learning is joyful when we connect with that wonderful creative energy and force.

R.S.: What do you think kids need most in their homes and schools?

Bernie: I'd say love. I also think we need to train parents. Bringing up kids is difficult. We brought up five children when my wife and I were still kids. I made plenty of noise and plenty of mistakes. Since then, I've apologized to our children and told them, "Hey, I'm sorry. What did I know?"

One day our oldest son said to me, "How come the younger ones don't have to do what I did?"

I responded, "Jonathan, I've learned that wasn't important."

I recently found a 22-year-old journal of mine. In it, I'd written about my concerns about not being a good father, but that our children would turn out okay because they were great kids. I copied it and mailed it to all five, with a note that they are great.

R.S.: You've written about the lessons people have learned from a life-threatening illness. What are some of those lessons that can be shared with people who haven't had such an experience?

Bernie: I was just thinking about a man, Peter Noll, who kept a journal called *Reflections on Death and Dying.* He wrote it when he learned he had a short time to live. One of the things he said was that you begin to realize time isn't money—time is everything. He said you realize that spending time with the things and people you love really becomes the most important thing in your life. They begin to live in the moment, so they're not always in the past or the future, worrying or reliving. They learn to make use of this moment, enjoying it and accepting it. And that's why a lot of people see their disease or their mortality as a gift because it gets them to start living. They start spending more time with the people and things they love.

Most of us are busy saying, "Someday my day will come," or "I'll get around to that," or "When I retire," and that really isn't the answer. Happiness is something internal. One must be grateful for life in order to be happy. And if you see life as a chance to contribute in a loving way to the world, then again, your life becomes meaningful so that each day you get up and give love to the world. It's as if the disease gives you permission to start living.

I started giving out buttons, and I think everyone should. Every teacher, parent, and adult figure should carry a pocket full of buttons that say, "You Make A Difference." When I meet people that make a difference in my life, I hand them a pin. I say, "Thank you, you've made a difference in my life, and I hope you'll pass this on to someone who has made a difference in your life."

R.S.: Bernie, you emanate joy in your being, in your speaking, and in your writing. What brought you to becoming the kind of healer that you are today?

Bernie: Well, my own pain. I don't think anyone really finds the joy until they first live through the pain. I would like to say this. A lot of times, people will say to me, "You're an optimist, so that's why you are the way you are." I always reply to them that I am not an optimist; I am a realist. As a realist, I know that I will run into many things that will cause grief and sorrow for me, but I am choosing to be joyful because I know what life is like. Amidst the sorrow and grief, I am choosing joy.

Now when you say, "What made me that individual?" I would say my pain as a physician, not being able to cure everybody, not knowing how to help people through their difficulties. So many of my patients have also been my teachers.

R.S.: Can you describe some of the most significant lessons that you've learned in your own life?

Bernie: I believe we are here to love, that we are really here to work on our own lives, and that if we all straighten out our own lives, then the world will become a much better place.

I believe we are here to revere all life. I really like to refer people back to nature. We need to learn from nature. I think we really have to give the same reverence to every form of life. Then the planet becomes a wonderful place.

R.S.: What are your greatest moments as a teacher these days?

Bernie: Emily Dickinson said in a poem, "If I can keep one heart from breaking, I shall not live in vain. If I can ease one life the aching or cool one pain, or help one fainting robin unto his nest again, I shall not live in vain."

So my greatest satisfaction these days comes from just helping people. If I help a human being get through an illness or the death of a loved one, then my life has meaning. To me, if you love, the ripples go out. I get letters from all over the world because I wrote a book and it traveled; my word travels, and we touch each other. I think anybody who sets out to love makes a difference in the world.

R.S.: What do you like the most? Is it the writing, the speaking, or the interviews?

Bernie: Interacting with people. I don't like the traveling, sitting on airplanes, or sleeping in strange hotels. I do like the people, and they come because they already know the message. In a sense, you can say that we are preaching to the already changed or the believers. But they are still struggling with life or the meaning of life. So when we get together, wonderful things happen.

I know a teacher who developed cancer and shared her experience with her class. She said that she began to notice that when she sat down for lunch duty, which she also began to enjoy and even do for other teachers, a lot of the so-called delinquents in the school came to eat lunch with her. She finally asked them why they were all eating lunch with her. They began to tell her how much they had learned from her, and they wanted to keep learning and be near her. They learned from her sharing her own pain and her own difficulty.

I was in a school where the principal said to me that I really needed to watch myself because it was dangerous. And I said to him, "Don't worry, I'll take care of myself. I'm not afraid to be here." I spoke to several combined

classes. While the students were coming in, they avoided four seats right in front of me. I thought maybe they were afraid of me and they wanted to sit in the back. Then four boys came in and plopped down in those seats. Halfway through my talk, I started asking questions. One of the boys in the front raised his hand. "What is it?" I said. When he answered, I said, "No, that's not the answer I'm looking for."

We went on, and by the end of the day, I learned that he was the gang leader of the entire school and that he had never spoken in high school. Finally he speaks, and I tell him he's wrong. The staff felt that he would never raise his hand again. I thought that they had missed the point. I had him involved and interested enough so that he *wanted* to raise his hand and say something, and he wasn't offended because I said no. He was still interested and participating.

Teachers have incredible power in the acceptance and love of their students. It has nothing to do with liking their behavior.

When somebody says, "I love you," most people don't know what to do. A while ago, I said that to a teenager who was screaming at me because of traffic. I happened to be in my car in front of him, and he was shouting obscenities, screaming at me, and even came up to my car window. I said to him, "I love you." Well, he ran back to his car and turned up another street. I think it upset him to have me say that, and I expected it would. I said it to make him think and feel. I just knew that it would disturb him more than if I screamed at him.

R. S.: Who have your greatest teachers been?

Bernie: I must say myself, and I don't mean that in an egotistical way. But I think that my pain has been my greatest teacher. A long time ago, I made the decision to try and be a loving person, so the person I'm most unhappy with is me, and the person who has taught me the most is me. Next are my wife Bobbie, our children, and my parents. The people we live with are our teachers and creators. Then I would also add people like Carl Jung, Joseph Campbell, Ashley Montagu, Erich Fromm, William Saroyan, Thornton Wilder, and I could go on and on.

R.S.: What's your best teacher story?

Teaching & Joy

Bernie: I was a very good student, skipped a couple of grades, and went to college when I was 16 years old. Socially, I think that was very difficult for me, but I still had a good time and did well.

In New York, we had the Regent's Exams. One of my teachers said, "You'll never get 100 percent on anything."

And I said, "Why not?"

He responded, "Because you are always in a hurry. You are always done first." And he was right. I would always get 95 percent. I would make a simple mistake and not go back and check and take my time.

I've also been thinking about the role of struggle and even failure as a teacher. Last night, I was reading about a man who wanted to be a writer. He got an idea to start a magazine in Spanish. When he asked, "Who knows the most about opportunities in South America?" someone gave him the name of a Mr. Watson, who happened to be the head of IBM. Not knowing this, the young man called up and said he would like to take Mr. Watson to lunch. He asked if they could meet at the zoo since he didn't have much money and wanted to buy Mr. Watson a sandwich. Instead, the secretary gave the young man an appointment.

As he got to the building, and went from one secretary to another, he realized he was in trouble. He went into Watson's office, which was bigger than the young man's home.

Watson said, "When you called and wanted information, it reminded me of myself when I was a young man, and I thought, why not talk to you."

"What do you want to be?" Watson asked.

"I want to be a writer, but I keep getting rejections."

Watson asked him how many rejections he had on his desk. When the man said 12, Watson said that wasn't enough.

"What do you mean that's not enough?"

"You have to fail many, many more times because you can learn from your failures. If you want to be a writer, sit down, look at why you've been rejected, and learn from it. You ought to have at least 10 rejections a week if you're really going to accomplish anything."

R.S.: If you were a new parent today and could start all over again, knowing all that you've been able to gather in this life, what would you teach your children?

Bernie: If I were a parent today, I would touch my child often because that lets children know that they are loved and it also changes them physically. I would repeat, "I love you" to that child. I would instill discipline, not punishment. I would also keep saying to that child that I'm not perfect as a parent. I've never had lessons, so if something comes up and I'm not doing it right, help me out or forgive me. When problems occur, I'd also say to the child what my mother used to say to me: "God is redirecting you. Something good will come of this." Norman Vincent Peale's mother used to say to him, "Norman, if God slams one door, further down the corridor, another one will be opened."

It doesn't matter if you get a disease or lose some money or if you're fired from a job. You step back, take a breath, and say, "Okay, what can I do with this? How can I use this?" To take this one step further, a man at one of our workshops who was diagnosed with cancer was shouting, "Why me?"

I asked him, "If you won the state lottery, what would you say?"

He said, "What can I do with it?" I told him to reverse the answers.

That's what you have to do with your life. When you confront an affliction or adversity, say, "What can I do with it?" That's what I would teach my children. If something wonderful happens, fine. But if something doesn't happen that you're thrilled about, you still step back and ask, "What can I do with this?" It is sad when people are told that they have a year to live and then say, "Now I can move, quit my job, deal with love, and change my life because I only have a year to live." You shouldn't need cancer to give yourself permission to live.

That's why I feel that our health and mortality also relate to self-esteem and love. I mean, if you don't love living, what's the point of being told about healthy diets and exercise? The gratitude has to come from within. You need self-esteem, self-love, and self-worth—then you can do all of the rest. Love the world in the way that makes you happy.

R.S.: A lot of parents and educators are dealing with the pace of change in the world these days. What are your thoughts on that?

Bernie: Change is a part of life, so I expect things to change, and maybe that's why I accept it. It's ridiculous to try to get things to not change; you can't stop it. So that's why I say look at nature. You see, in a biological system, if there is no change, it is terribly dangerous to the system. Suppose your heart always beats 70 times per minute and all of a sudden something disturbs it. You could die. But if your heart is used to changing, then you can deal with that change in a heartbeat. Biological systems are not consistent because the ability to change is healthier than a rigid, fixed system that never changes. We need chaos in life.

R.S.: Are there changes going on in your life?

Bernie: Yes, I'm constantly learning. I age; I change; I'm going through a process. Life is an evolution filled with confronting your own mortality and all of the things that go with that. Jung said, "The future is unconsciously prepared long in advance." I know that I'm creating my future by the decisions I am making every single day.

It may sound funny, but I know that one of the things that I have to learn is the ability to say no and to stop doing some of the things and to really start taking care of myself. I don't mean that I'm not taking care of myself, but I'm learning to take more time to just paint a picture or write a poem, rather than going out speaking and lecturing.

R.S.: So you're struggling to find your balance just like the rest of us?

Bernie: That's why I think I'm helpful to other people—because I'm dealing with the same things that they're dealing with.

R.S.: If you could, what prescription would you write for our schools?

Bernie: I think we already ask too much of the schools. I think the schools and the teachers have taken on a burden that in many ways is not fair and is the result of poor family environment and social problems. I would ask the schools to work on the self-esteem and self-worth of every student, and to

teach students how to educate themselves rather than to rely on the efforts of others. And I would ask schools not to have everybody evaluated by a grade. Instead of having a high-risk class, why not have a high-hopes class? When we take students who have learning differences, let's not label them as failures. Let's focus on the high hopes we have for their future. Remember, I said educate, not instruct.

At the end of the book *Babbit* by Sinclair Lewis, there is a story of a young man who decided not to go to college. Instead, he decided to marry his girlfriend and take a factory job. His family berated him. His father took him into the next room, and his message was, "You know, I have never done anything that I wanted to do in my life. Don't tell your mother that I said it, but I'm kind of proud of you for doing what you have done. The world is yours." Then, arm in arm, the Babbit men walked back to meet the family.

Now that's not an exact quote from the book, but I copied that page and sent it to each of our children. I think that when everybody shows up at school, they ought to get that page to see that you don't have to conform, you don't have to go to college, and you don't have to marry the "right" person. You just have to live your life and contribute to the world in your own way. And that's what I would ask teachers and parents to do for each child—help them find their own way. My parents did that for me. They didn't want me to be a doctor. They thought it would be a very tough and long road. They thought there were other ways they could have helped me more, but they never said, "Don't do it." They said, "If you want to do it, it's okay with us." My mother's answer was, "Do what will make you happy."

I had to deal with a similar situation with one of our sons. He was basically going to fail college because he didn't want to be there. So I stopped and said, "You don't have to go." After that, he went to innumerable schools to learn things that he was interested in, everything from electronics, to cars, to gardening.

Another of our children said he wanted to go to automotive school. This was our third child, so by now I'm getting a little smarter. I said, "Automotive school? You're very bright, why not college?" So what did he do? He went to automotive school. When he finished that, he went to college and got a law degree. Then he wrote for a publishing company that publishes automobile magazines and nostalgia magazines, and now he is a prosecuting attorney. He was also interested in models and toys. He earns his living doing the things he loves. I wish all children could earn their living at their hobby, at their joy, at what they played at as children. I gradually learned as we went down the line with our children to stop pressuring them to conform, and I love each one with all of my heart.

I send a monthly letter to our children, sharing things that touch and teach me from the present and our past. My children help me keep my feet on the ground. Upon learning I was to receive a prestigious award, one said, "I guess they've lowered their standards."

More recently, another asked if I was going to write another book. I said, "Maybe, 'Out of My Wit and Wisdom.'"

He said, "Call it, 'Out of My Mind.'" I plan to do just that. I have learned that life is a series of beginnings. We may have losses, but nothing really ever ends.

Bernie Siegel practiced general and pediatric surgery in New Haven, Connecticut, until he retired in 1989. In 1978, he started ECap (Exceptional Cancer Patients) to help patients in a loving, safe, therapeutic confrontation that facilitates personal change and healing. Siegel travels extensively with his wife Bobbie, sharing his insights and experiences through workshops and lectures.

In 1988, Siegel became President of the American Holistic Medical Association. His books include Love, Medicine and Miracles; Peace, Love and Healing; *and his most recent success,* How to Live Between Office Visits.

Reverence for children is reverence for life. Shinichi Suzuki, known to many as the originator of the Suzuki approach to music instruction, has demonstrated reverence for children throughout his life. This story captures a moment of that respect.

24

The Heart Radiates

BY SHINICHI SUZUKI

I was lecturing at a small kindergarten in the Kansai Area. After the lecture I sat in the middle of the front row in the room while listening to the children give a concert. Just then, a barefooted beggar child of 6 or 7 came to my side and confronted me. I invited him to sit in the empty seat next to me so that we could listen together. The child nodded in acceptance and listened quietly.

At the end of one piece, I clapped and said to the child, "Good, aren't they?" The child clapped, too, and returned my smile with a laugh. He listened to the next piece, quietly also. I asked him if it was interesting and he said, while he clapped, that it was very interesting.

Source: Excerpted from *Ability Development from Age Zero* by Shinichi Suzuki. Translated by Mary Louise Nagata. Reprinted by permission of Shinichi Suzuki.

After the concert ended, the kindergarten teachers expressed surprise. That child, who often sneaked into the kindergarten to play with the children, was the child of a wandering tramp. The word spread.

"That child cannot settle down. He cannot concentrate upon one thing. He often gets in the way so I have to put him out. What could have happened today?"

"I saw the child sit right next to Mr. Suzuki and he sat down until the end. He even clapped his hands."

It was not miraculous. The child could feel my radiations of respect for children, and when I spoke to him with praise and interest, he was happy to be treated as an equal human being. The attitude of the child changed because the way in which he was treated changed. Instead of being treated as a pest, he was treated as an equal. It was easy for the child to sit for an hour because it was fun.

The heart radiations, and the thoughts and feelings of a person, show all over. The ragamuffin in Suwa probably had no mother. He was only a barefoot tramp in rags. Even a child of such an environment could feel the wonderfulness of human life. A child has so much ability.

Reverence for children is reverence for life.

Shinichi Suzuki was born in Nagoya, Japan, in October 1898. He is known throughout the world as the founder of the Talent Education Movement, the most visible aspect of which has been the musical training of very young children to a high degree of proficiency on a string instrument or piano.

Suzuki has dedicated his life to improving educational methods. Convinced that enthusiasm to learn can be sustained indefinitely if the teaching method is correct, he appealed for early education "from age zero" long before modern psychologists popularized the idea.

His interest in education subsequently resulted in the formation of the Early Development Association in Japan, which continues research into the learning abilities of what we know as the preschool child. Since 1964, he has

made repeated visits to the United States and Canada to work with teachers and students and to talk to parents about the education of their children.

Every day, we're given an opportunity to share our joy and practice an attitude of gratitude. Will you?

25

Forty-Nine Years Later

BY AL FIALKA

My story has a happy ending. I was sitting in church one day, sort of half-listening to the sermon. Then, certain spoken words caught my attention, and I began to listen more closely. The minister was saying, "Too many of us let life go on and we don't take an active part in it like we should. Things happen to us, we feel and we think, and then we wait for the next day to come." The words from the pulpit kept coming and now I was alert, waiting for more. "We all have certain people who touched our lives in one way or another, such as a friend, counselor, boss, nurse, or teacher. Have we ever told them how we feel?"

A teacher who touched my life? Sure, I had one, my 9th grade algebra teacher—and that was 49 years ago—but I've never forgotten her. I've mentioned her to other people many times because she showed me self-confidence, a pleasant manner, and respect for other people. She was one of my favorite role models. Although many people have come into my life, I've never forgotten her name or what she did for me. That sermon asked: "Why don't we ever tell these people how we feel about them?" I knew I should tell her how I feel, but how, after 49 years?

I write a newspaper column for various papers in our area and decided to mention the theme of the sermon in one of my columns, along with the name of the teacher who had meant so much to me, Miss Irene Lemke. I also mentioned that I had no idea where she was at this time. Fortunately, one of our thoughtful readers wrote me a note saying that Miss Lemke was in a rest home after suffering a stroke. I just had to see her.

A few days later, I stopped at a florist and picked up a small bouquet. I drove out to the rest home and went up to Miss Lemke's room. She was lying on her bed, and the nurse said she couldn't speak but she could hear and understand. Miss Lemke looked just as neat and prim as I remembered, with eyes filled with warmth. I thought she was beautiful. She was still an inspiration—little wonder that I had never forgotten her. I told her who I was and how I felt about what she had come to mean to me. She looked at me, her eyes sparkled, and tears rolled down her cheeks. I kissed her on the forehead. She couldn't move. I touched her shoulder. She smiled. Tears came into my own eyes, and I found it difficult to breathe past the swelling in my throat. I held her hand as I softly waved goodbye. The next day I learned that she had passed away during the night. Having waited 49 years, how very lucky I was—how very thankful I am—that I had the chance to tell her how her teaching had affected me. If I had waited just one more day, it would have been too late. Don't *you* wait 49 years!

Al Fialka was born in Flint, Michigan, one of 11 children. He has lived in Flint his entire life. During World War II, he fought in Europe and was injured in France. Fialka graduated from the University of Michigan in 1950. He is a retired finance administrator for the Buick Motor Division, where he worked 30 years. Married 48 years, Fialka and his wife Dolores have 4 children and 6 grandchildren.

For the past 12 years, Fialka has written a newspaper column "Observations on Life" and often freelances articles for various newspapers in Michigan.

An Invitation

Despite much of what we hear in the current political debate about U.S. education, we have much for which to be thankful. We have many wonderful schools and teachers. We are educating an incredibly diverse student population and consistently achieving higher standardized test scores and graduation rates. We have classrooms where joy is always present. Occasionally, we find whole schools where joy is part of the curriculum.

We have millions of parents who support their children and their schools. How privileged we are to work with their children.

Of course, we need to improve our schools. Our economy and culture have changed. Technology is changing. As good as schools are, we need to improve.

For all those who strive to improve our schools, we have a reminder and an invitation. Like wonderful teachers who strive to improve the hearts and minds of their students, those of us who strive to improve our schools will be successful if we are skilled educators, if we work together, and if our hearts are filled with joy and respect for schools and teachers and parents and students.

If you have stories about great learning and its relationship to joy, please consider joining us in our next publication. Send your stories or ideas to

Bob Sornson	Jim Scott
5184 Milroy Lane	4986 Country Manor
Brighton, MI 48116	Jackson, MI 49201

About the Editors

Jim Scott is a professor at Jackson Community College in Jackson, Michigan. He has worked in the areas of wellness, stress management, and parenting skills for more than 20 years. Scott's areas of interest educationally and professionally are related to building community in the classroom and creating experientially based learning opportunities. He actively serves his community and speaks frequently promoting the concepts of empowerment and healthy living. Scott and his wife Lisa have three terrific children, with whom they pursue life's adventures.

Bob Sornson is the Executive Director of Special Education Services for Northville Public Schools, Northville, Michigan. He has been an educator for more than 20 years. Sornson has many interests, including learning about the incredible diversity of thinking and learning styles; parenting; the relationship between motoric and cognitive development; preventing learning problems; developing the habits of lifetime learning; and living with joy. Sornson writes and consults. His four children and wife nurture his spirit and help him discover joy.